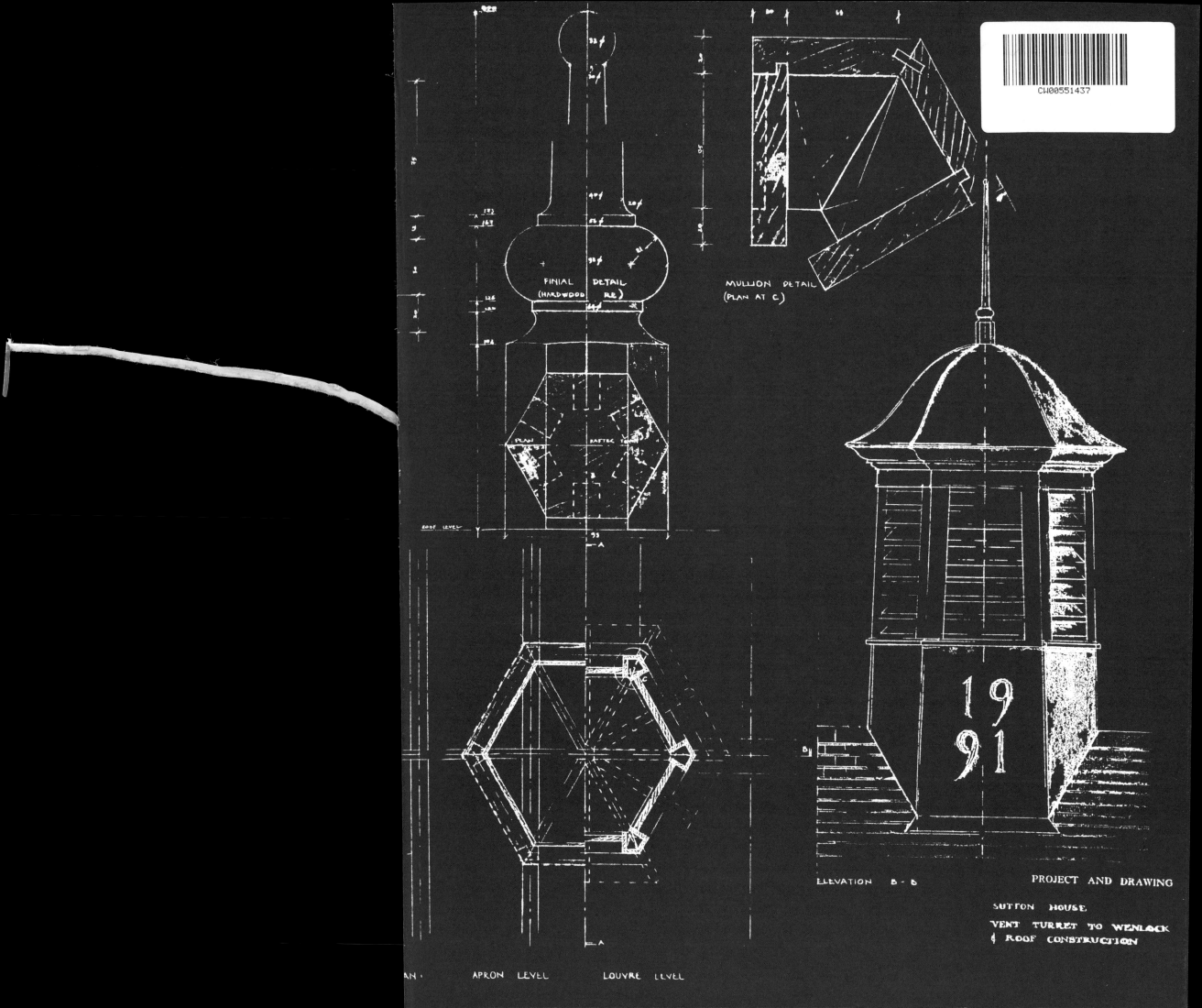

FINIAL DETAIL
(HARDWOOD RE)

MULLION DETAIL
(PLAN AT C)

ROOF LEVEL

19
91

ELEVATION B - B

PROJECT AND DRAWING

SUTTON HOUSE
VENT TURRET TO WENLOCK
& ROOF CONSTRUCTION

APRON LEVEL   LOUVRE LEVEL

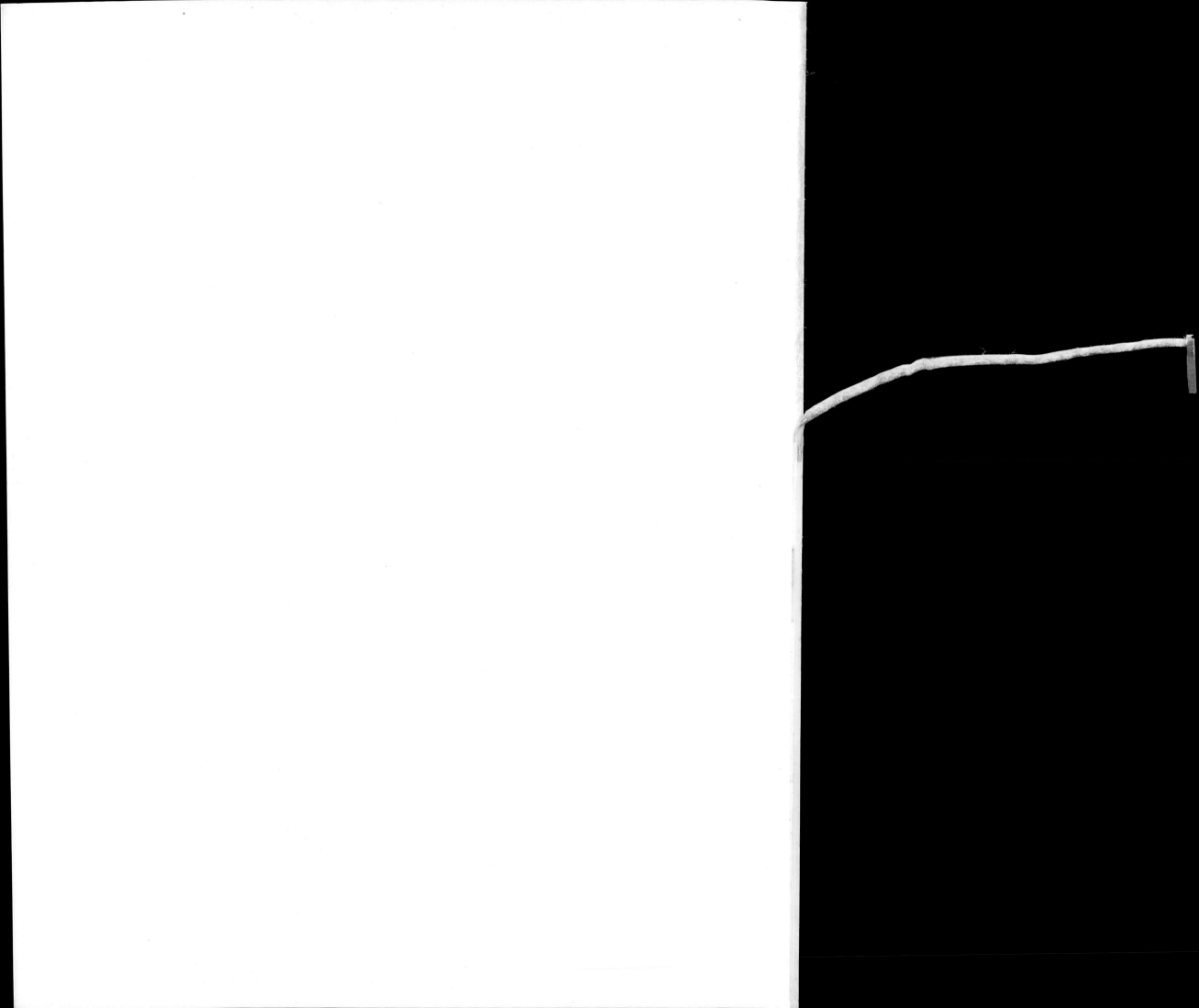

OLD
BVILDINGS
NEW
ARCHITECTVRE

OLD BUILDINGS, NEW ARCHITECTURE

The work of Richard Griffiths Architects

Richard Griffiths

Publication

First published in the United Kingdom in 2019 by Richard Griffiths Architects

Designed by Richard Griffiths Architects

© Richard Griffiths Architects

Cataloguing-in British Library Publication Data

A catalogue record for this book is available from the British Library

ISBN 978-1-5272-3162-7

'Stoneface' typeface courtesy Eric R. Kuhne & The Princeton Architectural Press, after stone inscriptions designed by Leon Battista Alberti.

'Whitney' typeface designed by Tobias Frere-Jones for New York's Whitney Museum.

Printed by Henry Ling, Dorchester.

Image credits

AHMM: p. 87
Arup: p. 165
Richard Boad: p. 23
Christina Chelmick: pp. 40, 41, 42, 43
Chapman Taylor: p. 165
Peter Cook: p. 169
Stuart Davis: p. 152
Dave Dunford: p. 12
Dominic French: p. 53
Dennis Gilbert: pp. 13, 14, 15, 17, 26, 28, 29-30, 31, 32, 33, 34, 35, 36, 37, 38, 39, 62, 63, 64, 67, 68, 69, 70, 106, 108, 109, 142, 143, 174.
Michael Heffernan: p. 10
Charles Hosea: p. 85
Hufton & Crow: pp. 156, 158, 160, 162, 163.
Alana Johnson/Currier Museum of Art: p. 89
Gemma Klein: p. 140-141
Andy Marshall: pp. 54, 58, 59, 60.
Guy Montagu-Pollock: p. 112
James Morris: pp. 5, 18, 22, 23.
Rufus Owen: p. 95
Price & Myers: p. 71
Will Pryce: pp. 8, 46, 47, 49, 72, 74, 75, 76-77, 79, 80, 110, 114, 145, 146, 147.
Daniel Shearing: pp. 81, 82-83.
Dan Smith: pp. 96, 102.
Grant Smith: p. 170
Morley von Sternberg: p. 49
Urdang Academy: p. 80
Simon Withers: p. 57

Covers

Front cover and title page
Lambeth Palace
Our courtyard bridge between the medieval Chapel and Blore's Palace.

Front endpaper
Sutton House
Drawing for the new ventilation turret on Wenlock Barn.

Rear endpaper
St Albans Abbey
Drawing for the choir stall alterations.

Rear cover
Sutton House
Preserved cobwebs in the Tudor privy off the Victorian Parlour.

This book is dedicated

to the teachers who taught me and to the architects for whom I worked;

to the clients, consultants and craftsmen with whom we have enjoyed collaboration;

to the members of Richard Griffiths Architects, past and present;

to all who assisted in the production of this book;

and to my wife and family for their constant support and encouragement.

Contents

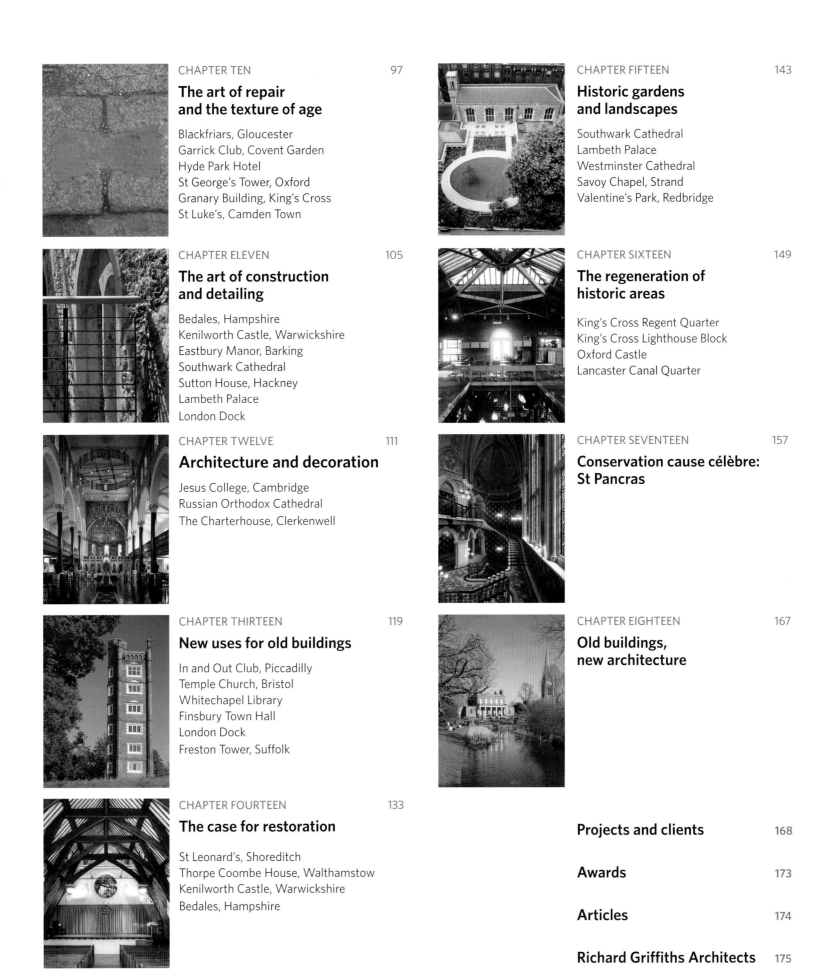

Preface

Architecture aims at eternity.
Christopher Wren, *Parentalia,* Of Architecture

An easy commerce of the old and the new,
The complete consort dancing together.
TS Eliot, *Four Quartets,* Little Gidding

This is an account of architecture that relates to old buildings rather than to new. Architecture is the same demanding mistress whether one is working with new buildings or with old, and the eternal verities of architecture – form, function, construction – apply when working with old and new buildings alike. However old buildings also embody the attributes of age and of memory, and the architect who works with old buildings has the challenge of understanding their history and significance, of engaging with all the historic layers that are already present, and of adding a new architectural layer. Old buildings define a sense of place as carriers of memory, palimpsests waiting to be over-written. The architect working with old buildings engages with them in an intimate relationship, and aims, as TS Eliot put it, *to achieve an easy commerce of the old and the new, the complete consort dancing together.*

The Roman architect Vitruvius defined the elements of architecture as Commoditas, Firmitas and Venustas, famously translated by Wotton as Commodity, Firmness and Delight. These three elements remain as the foundation of architecture, albeit expressed more appropriately today as Function, Construction and Beauty. Functional considerations have largely shaped architecture since the early 20th century, and the Modern Movement's emphasis on Function has too often been at the expense of Beauty. Meanwhile, those architects working on old buildings are increasingly called Conservation Architects, and treated as mere specialists in the Technical aspects of repair, and of achieving statutory consents for historic buildings. In neither field does the idea of Beauty get much of a look in, and I remember being surprised as a student – of both architecture and conservation – that Beauty was practically never mentioned. Yet architecture has the ability to move people just as much as literature, music or art.

Opposite
Russian Orthodox Cathedral
New chandeliers incorporating the Greek Cross.

This book is my record of a lifetime searching for Beauty in architecture, through interaction with buildings of all periods and all types, adding a new layer to the historic layers that are already present. It describes the detective work involved in discovering and understanding the history of the buildings, their memories and significance. It describes the process of revealing the best of the old, and providing for the needs of the new, through a creative dialogue between past, present and future.

The message of my book is that old buildings provide fertile ground for the creation of new architecture, enriching the lives of those living today and in the future.

CHAPTER ONE

The making of an architect

An architect should be a good writer, a skilful draftsman, versed in geometry and optics, expert at figures, acquainted with history, informed on the principles of natural and moral philosophy, somewhat of a musician, not ignorant of the sciences both of law and physic.
Vitruvius, *De Architectura,* c20 BCE

Architecture is frozen music.
Goethe, *Conversations with Eckermann,* 1829

It took me a long time to find my direction in life, in which my talents – which lay more in the sciences – and my interests – which lay more in the arts – might be happily married. At school I studied maths and physics, and I went up to Cambridge to study engineering. I found escape from its excessively technical focus through singing and playing music. In retrospect, the sublime conjunction of great music and great architecture helped me to find my eventual direction – Bach's B Minor Mass in King's College Chapel, the Berlioz Requiem in Ely Cathedral, the Mozart Requiem in Saint Germain-des-Près.

Opposite
The author at Sutton House in 1988

Right
Dalibor Vesely drew this sketch during a tutorial about a design project for Kentish Town, evoking possibilities for urban development around a communal garden at the centre of each urban block.

My Damascene moment came at 3am one morning when I woke with a start and realised that I wanted to become an architect. I started again, in 1974, from the beginning, but always with the view that I wanted to work at the interface between old and new in Architecture. It is to Dalibor Vesely that I owe the beginnings of an ability to relate my interest in old buildings to the design of new buildings. Dalibor had revolutionised teaching at the Architectural Association in the days of Alvin Boyarsky, and had launched a similar revolution at Cambridge, bringing a new continental, urban and cultural sensibility to a school that had been excessively focused on the properties of built form. I treasure a sketch of Dalibor's from one of my early tutorials, drawn by him while discussing the possible components of the brief – a concert hall, apartments, a genetic research laboratory and a monastery for Kentish Town (with a population, as Dalibor pointed out, the same as that of medieval Siena). His pencil never stopped moving, and its faint traces conjured up infinite possibilities in defiance of the determinism of the Modern Movement.

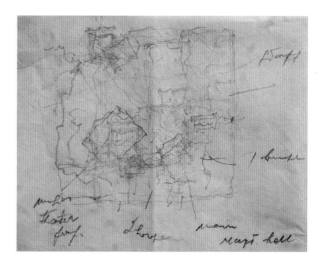

My first experience in practice was with Fred Burn (of Frederick Burn, Smith and Partners) who looked after a number of stately homes saved by the Mutual Households Association from the fate of demolition that awaited so many houses in the immediate post-war years, by conversion to retirement apartments – Gosfield Hall (Tudor), Swallowfield Park (Georgian), Aynhoe Park (Archer and Soane), Great Maytham (Lutyens). The satisfaction of witnessing the finished product of my work confirmed me in my chosen field of architecture.

However, I wanted to gain experience of new building first, and moved back to Cambridge to work with Christophe Grillet (of Lyster, Grillet and Harding) on Clive Sinclair's Research Headquarters at Milton Hall, just north of Cambridge, which he had just purchased. It was a delirious roller coaster, with drawings that we issued one day being built the next.

Milton Hall was followed by the conversion of the former County Hall on Hobson Street for Christ's College. The former offices were converted to form groups of six rooms sharing a kitchen and bathroom, very popular with the students, and the former Council Chamber on the top floor was converted to an auditorium approached by a new glazed external stair. The chairman of the building subcommittee, an eminent physicist, requested a sample of the proposed type of glass. At the next meeting he reported that he had carried out tests at the Cavendish laboratories, and had calculated that at noon on a sunny day in mid-July the temperature might reach 130F and did we think that was acceptable? We went away to carry out a major redesign.

I moved back to London to work with Anthony Blee at the Sir Basil Spence Partnership. Anthony had been Spence's assistant at Coventry Cathedral, and was a fount of wonderful stories about the Spence office, which he would act out in inimitable style. As well as re-designing Moss Bros in Covent Garden, I would deliver drawings, photos and papers to him at the latest Planning Inquiry where he was acting as Expert Witness. Many years later we were both involved at a Planning Inquiry about the refusal of consent for the demolition of the Victorian wings of the Georgian Barrington Park in Gloucerstershire. The site visit was unforgettable. Following sandwiches in the kitchen, apparently the last refuge of the squire and his wife, we went for the site visit: leather bound books crawling with lice in a trunk in the servants' hall; slime on curtains collapsing from the rails of damp-sodden bedrooms; and a large chunk of the elaborate plaster ceiling of the magnificent Palladian saloon lying in a depression in the middle of the carpet, where it had sat for at least ten years. The squire had, however, kept the estate intact- mansion, park, parish church and two whole villages - throughout the post-War period when country houses were being demolished every week.

Top left
Great Maytham, *Rolvenden, Kent was built to designs by Lutyens in 1911. My first project was to rebuild the collapsing south terrace and steps leading to the garden.*

Top right
Barrington Park, *Gloucesterhire, was notorious in the 1970's for the neglect of the house and estate including the parish church and two villages. These have now been repaired, including the Victorian wings added by McVicar Anderson to the Palladian house of 1740.*

Bottom left
Milton Hall, *a country house outside Cambridge, was converted to headquarters offices and research laboratories for Sir Clive Sinclair. A new colonnade of a primitive timber Doric Order screens the wings added in the 1960's.*

A few months after I started with Anthony Blee, I received, out of the blue, an invitation to interview from Julian Harrap. I had written to him when I moved to London in 1986 because I admired his work at the SPAB headquarters in Spital Square with its lead-clad, Mackintosh-inspired gable window. Julian was unique for an architect specialising in the conservation field, having worked for James Stirling, initially as a model-maker. He had made a conscious decision to work with old buildings, finding it to be a field in which the odds were stacked more favourably towards the creation of Architecture than in the field of new building. This was due to the beneficial presence of a carrot – the availability of grant aid - and a stick – the need for listed building consent. Having cut his teeth on rebuilding the houses in Spitalfields saved by Dan Cruickshank, Mark Girouard and others following the battle of Elder Street, Julian had become the pre-eminent architect working on historic buildings in East London.

Julian had previously only taken on architects unsullied by working for others, and my interview took the form of visits to two of his projects to gauge my reaction. The first was to Teulon's St Mark's Silvertown, burnt out in a fire, where the re-roofing with a continental chevron pattern of grey and green Westmoreland slates, and the picking out of the chamfers of the rebuilt trusses in red, made a great aesthetic impact. We then climbed the tower of Hawksmoor's St Anne's Limehouse, stepped into the roofspace and switched on the lights. Rarely have I received an aesthetic thrill more acute, the alternation of PC Hardwick's timber trusses and Julian's new steel trusses painted in a blue-grey colour suddenly revealed in light. Technically the design was brilliant too, the new trusses having been inserted piece by piece into the roofspace and then bolted together, without any scaffolding or propping. Their weight was no greater than that of the slates of the bay of the roof that had been removed. This was an Architecture to which I could relate, combining old and new, and harnessing technical ingenuity to aesthetic ends. I felt that I had arrived.

Bliss was it in that dawn to be alive. Each day I would cycle to the office behind a Turkish watchmaker's just north of Dalston, then a byword for gang warfare among the Yardies, and enter via a yard shared with an incontinent dog. From here we would plot the saving of historic buildings in East London, almost all in an advanced state of dereliction, and all having the rich character of age, texture, weathering and decay that, at best, gave them a sublime beauty. Their dereliction also meant that they had not suffered alteration in recent years, and that their layers of history and alteration remained intact to be uncovered, like a forensic excavation, as a basis for planning their renewal.

The Old Dispensary, Romford Road, Stratford

My first project at Julian Harrap's was the repair and conversion of the Old Dispensary on Romford Road as offices for the Passmore Edwards Museum service in Newham. I had inherited a feasibility study for the repair of the building - similar to the typical New England five-bay farmhouse – when suddenly funding became available. The project involved repairing and converting the mid-Georgian clapboarded, timber framed, house to offices, and building a new rear extension containing kitchens and lavatories. I designed the extension as a subliminally classical building sitting below the cornice of the Georgian rear elevation, containing kitchens and WC's linked by a vertical tall window between giant order pilasters. The extension allowed the Georgian house with its timber frame and its panelling to be restored and refitted as offices without subdivision.

It was extraordinary that the Georgian building should have been standing at all. The timber sole plate had rotted away entirely; the ends of the timber studs had been sawn off and were supported by piles of unbonded bricks; and the corner post had been cut off and removed to a height of four feet above ground level with nothing supporting it apart from the nails in the clapboarding. The project provided a wonderful learning experience about the repair of timber structures, and about the language of Georgian detailing with its timber panelling and applied skirting, dado, and four-part timber cornice. It was also an object lesson about how crucial the design of heating and lighting is to the aesthetic whole. We had chosen electric radiant heating panels above the ceiling as an invisible and economic solution in conjunction with full insulation of the timber frame. Unfortunately, the plaster finish was applied to metal lath rather than to plaster lath, and at a very late stage in the contract a workman received an electric shock from touching the metal architrave bead between the door frame and the light switch. I had to convene a meeting to explain how all those around the table could be held negligent if the

matter went to court, and proposed that the only solution was to abandon the existing installation entirely, and to replace it with radiant heating panels under the wooden floorboards instead, everyone bearing their own costs in the matter. Fortunately, I succeeded in getting everyone to agree.

Top
The Old Dispensary *in its derelict state in 1988.*

Bottom
The Georgian timber-framed building was rescued from dereliction and converted to office use. The extension contains a kitchen and a pair of toilets on each floor, flanking a double height window to the lobby between. By means of opening doors and shutters, the ground floor lobby and WC's can be combined to create a single accessible toilet.

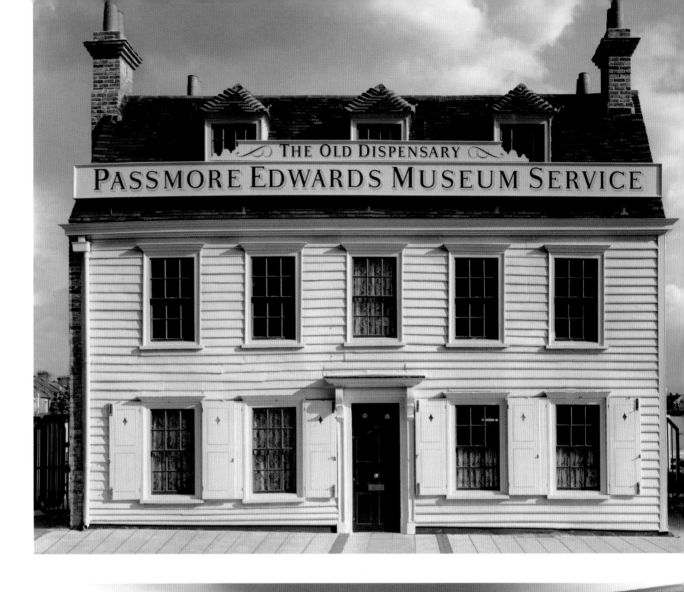

Top
The Old Dispensary *was in a state of near collapse when it was saved by its repair and conversion to museum offices.*

Bottom
The meeting room on the ground floor after repair.

The Ragged School Museum

The Ragged School Museum, on the canal just north of the Limehouse Basin, was founded by Tom Ridge, a remarkable local school teacher who realised that these canalside warehouses were once the largest Ragged School in London. The Ragged Schools, founded by Dr Barnardo, reached the poorest of the East End children because they, unlike the state primary schools, provided free lunch. I became architect for the conversion of the smaller of the warehouses into what is now the Ragged School Museum. This building allows schoolchildren to learn about the conditions suffered by the poorest children in Victorian East London, and the education that they received. It incorporates a reconstructed Victorian classroom on the first floor, exhibits and a Victorian parlour kitchen on the top floor, and a small canalside café at the lowest level. The main concern was to protect the floors and stairs in the case of fire. We achieved this by applying a fireproof lining below the floorboards and between the joists, which were treated with intumescent paint. This swells in the case of fire and protects the timber from charring. The main beams did not require intumescent protection, since even when charred they would be structurally sound. In this manner the original wooden floorboard joists and beams could be left exposed to view at each floor level.

The project was completed in 1988, and, remarkably, we were re-appointed nearly 30 years later to convert the larger of the two warehouses, the original Ragged School of 1877, into an extension of the Museum. The project will make the whole building accessible, extending museum use through the whole of the ground floor. It will also be able to generate an income from a fine toplit studio on the top floor, office workspace on the second floor, and a much enlarged café/ bar opening onto the canal. This should ensure its economic and social sustainability following the demise of local authority funding, and reveal its full historical and architectural interest.

Top
The Ragged School Museum, *Copperfield Road, Tower Hamlets was converted for use as a Ragged School from canalside warehouses shortly after it was built. I first converted no 48 to museum use in 1989, and returned to convert no 46 in 2017.*

Bottom
The recreated Victorian classroom was decorated in the original chocolate and primrose yellow stone colour. It has allowed generations of schoolchildren to experience the rigours of Victorian education.

Top
Ragged School Museum
*The floors were upgraded
by fireproofing between
the joists and applying
intumescent paint so
as to maintain the open
warehouse appearance.*

Bottom
*The ground floor entrance
with half hour fire
enclosure to the staircase
following the language of
the original panelling.*

CHAPTER TWO

The layering of history: Sutton House

Sir Ralph Sadleir saw the interest of the state altered six times, and died an honest man; the crown was put upon four heads, yet he continued a faithful subject; religion changed five times, yet he kept his faith. He was a most excellent writer, and a most valiant soldier, a qualification that is seldom met, so great is the distance between the sword and the pen.
The historian Lloyd on Sir Ralph Sadleir, builder of Bryck Place, now Sutton House

When I started working with Julian Harrap in 1986, I had recently moved to Stoke Newington, joined the Hackney Society, and became involved with the remarkable group of people who had come together to form the Campaign to save Sutton House, the Tudor house in Hackney owned by the National Trust. The house had been acquired in the aftermath of the First World War by the National Trust acting in conjunction with the Society for the Protection of Ancient Buildings. The National Trust took it on without contents or endowment and had let it out as offices, latterly to the ASTMS trade union under Clive Jenkins, who had his office in the Tudor linenfold panelled room. After the ASTMS departed at short notice, the house was left empty, squatted, vandalised, and rotting fast, and the Trust decided that conversion to private flats was the only way to give it a viable future.

Opposite
Sutton House
The Victorian Parlour with 200-year old cobwebs carefully preserved in the Tudor Privy that was blocked up in the 18th century.

The Campaign proved to be a golden exemplar of community activism in achieving its aim: to persuade the owner of a historic building to retain it in public use and for public benefit. Mike Gray, a photographer, wrote the letter to the Hackney Gazette that brought together the members of the Campaign, became its figurehead, and devoted his life to researching the history of the house. Julia Lafferty organised a questionnaire and petition that demonstrated a degree of local interest that took the National Trust by surprise. Jane Straker masterminded the campaign to seek out supporters inside the National Trust and English Heritage. Ken Jacobs devoted his spare time to going through the dust under the floorboards and uncovered a wealth of social history, from mummified rats to Victorian leather gloves and girls' school exercises (Pepys visited Hackney church in 1667 in order to ogle 'the young ladies of the schools whereof there is great store, very pretty'). Carole Mills, House Manager for the National Trust, went way beyond the call of duty to make the Community Scheme and education project an enormous success. This led the National Trust into an innovative engagement with the local community in the inner city.

Nothing was known about Sutton House before its Edwardian incarnation as a Church Institute. It had been called Sutton House by the National Trust in the belief that it had been owned by Sir Thomas Sutton, the 'richest commoner in England' and founder of the Charterhouse. However, Mike Gray found a drawing in the Charterhouse archives proving that Sutton in fact owned the house next door. From these inauspicious beginnings, he uncovered the whole history of ownership of both halves of the house throughout its history, including its origins in the 1530's as Bryck Place, the first house of Sir Rafe Sadleir, right hand man to Thomas Cromwell, who owned Brooke House close by.

Sadleir is now more deservedly famous, thanks to Hilary Mantel's Wolf Hall, and his handsome features were identified by Mike Gray in a previously unidentified Holbein portrait.

Following its gradual descent from its origins as one of the richest villages in the kingdom in the 16th century to one of the most deprived boroughs in the country in the late 20th century, Hackney became a byword for inner city deprivation, Lower Clapton Road became known as 'murder mile' and Sutton House became abandoned and derelict, inhabited by squatters, pigeons and dry rot.

Sutton House's rich layering of social history was matched by an equally rich architectural history. Successive layers of alteration were superimposed on the past without obliterating it. Sutton House was built as a Tudor mansion, with oak panelling in the main rooms. In the 17th century the west stair was rebuilt with Jacobean wall paintings. In the 18th century the house was re-fronted with new panelled rooms and a fine East staircase with twisted balusters. In the 19th century, the western half became a girls' school and the eastern half became a house for Huguenot silk weavers, with a fine new Victorian Parlour on the first floor, and a newly rendered elevation. In the early 20th century the two halves were reunited to become a Church Institute, equipped with accommodation for the curates and facilities for the youth of the parish – billiard room, chapel and Wenlock Barn, a parish hall. In the late 20th century the House gained some fine squatters graffiti, and we discovered 200 year-old cobwebs in the Tudor privy that had been bricked up in the East wing. Every room carried the marks of its multi-layered social and architectural history.

Opposite, top
Sutton House *in
the 1980's – derelict,
vandalised and squatted.*

*Opposite, bottom
The multi-layered façade
of Sutton House showing
the Tudor wings with
chamfered corners, the
Georgian refacing of the
central hall range, the
Victorian refacing of
the east wing, and the
Edwardian porches leading
to my contemporary ash
and bronze entrance
screen.*

*Top left
Sutton House as it would
have appeared as built by
Sir Rafe Sadleir in 1535,
a date established by
dendrochronology. The
oak beams and joists
proved to be of English
oak freshly felled, but the
linenfold panelling was of
Baltic oak, imported for its
straight grain and capacity
to be split into thin panels.*

*Top right
The retrieved pieces of
panelling were fixed to a
vertical surface, rectified
photos taken, printed
and cut up as a jigsaw for
reassembly in the original
configuration.*

I found myself in the unique position of acting as architect to the local campaigners in planning the alternative Community Scheme. This featured an ambitious mix of historic house rooms open to the public, an education programme, a hall for concerts and talks, space for changing exhibitions, a shop and café. My design developed from debates about the purpose and approach with a group of passionate advocates, none of whom was the owner. We were determined that the house should retain the richness and multi-layered complexity of its social and architectural history, and that we should add a new layer of integrity and interest to all those already present.

My dilemma was how to find a way to do this without making a self-conscious display of the layers of history, turning the house into a museum object rather than a lived-in piece of architecture. My solution was to introduce hinged panels into the panelling and plastered surfaces to allow the integrity of the different historic layers to be enjoyed intact; when opened, these hinged panels reveal the survival of Tudor floors, walls, plaster, decoration and fireplaces in the layer below. In the whole house I introduced 43 hinged panels. These allow visitors a sense of discovery and excitement by revealing the complex story of construction and successive alteration.

The repair of the house was greatly complicated by its dereliction and decay, and by the theft and removal of the panelling which had been retrieved in many pieces, large and small, all unrecorded. We devised innovative ways to carry out repairs without destroying history, for example in the flitched steel lattice beam that was inserted into a channel cut by chain saw into the defective beam below the Great Chamber in order to allow the removal of the post in the middle of the room below; and in the glass panel inserted into the floor of the entrance lobby to the new WC's in order to reveal the historic Tudor privy below. The reconstruction of the panelling itself was planned by means of rectified photographs, cut up and reassembled like a jigsaw puzzle.

To the historic materials – the oak and iron of the Tudor house, and the painted softwood and brass of the Georgian alterations - I added a new contemporary layer of ash and bronze. This allowed my new layer of design to be distinguished from all the historic layers, in the entrance screen, in Wenlock Barn, and in the café bar extension, with its square grid of ash joists and ash banding that runs through the roof, walls and floor.

Top row
The Tudor layer of oak and iron: the linenfold panelled room was restored with hinged panels, wide oak boards and radiators hidden below slatted window seats.

Second row
The Georgian layer of painted softwood and brass: hinged panels in the Georgian Parlour reveal the Tudor wall finishes and the Tudor fireplace underneath.

Third row
The Victorian layer of painted plaster and bronze: The Victorian parlour was restored reusing the Victorian fireplace removed from the Georgian Parlour, and revealing the rediscovered Tudor privy.

Fourth row
The 1980's layer with squatters' graffiti in the Tudor kitchen and in the attic; and preserved cobwebs in the Tudor privy.

Bottom row
My contemporary layer of ash and bronze in the entrance screen, in the Edwardian Wenlock Barn, and in the new staircase to the office wing.

Loe and Company. Peter Loe and his small team of highly skilled craftsmen were dedicated to realising the opportunities and excitement offered by this unique project, notably the three Johns: John the bricklayer, John the joiner and John the plasterer.

Towards the end of the project the recession led in 1993 to my leaving Julian Harrap and setting up on my own in my back bedroom. The project at Sutton House went with me, and it became my passport to future work, not least thanks to English Heritage having their Christmas lunch there. I was extraordinarily fortunate to have been entrusted with a project of such richness and complexity at this formative period in my career.

Top
The new conservatory extension to the café/bar is designed as a three-dimensional grid of ash, embracing the walls, the floor, the ceiling rafters and the bar counter.

Upper right
The team that worked so happily together, Carole Mills (NT), the craftsmen from Loe and Co. and myself.

Lower right
Guiding a group tour of the Great Chamber.

The complex layering of social and architectural history was matched by an equally complex layering of use. I took it as a challenge to equip each room so that it could be used on different days of the week as either a historic room for visiting, as a base for education visits, or as a venue for functions or events. I re-fixed the cornice to the oak panelling with a small gap to allow picture hooks to be inserted, to memorable effect when the whole house was taken over for an exhibition of young Scottish artists. It was a joy to see Wenlock Barn used for concerts, especially a performance of Stravinsky's Soldier's Tale before work started, and the whole house taken over for the annual Craft Fair, first held in the derelict house in 1990 when nearly 1000 people visited. We were innovative in writing into the contract that the builder should open the site to visitors on two Saturdays during the contract, with the craftsmen demonstrating their work. I was fortunate to have wonderful builders from

Overleaf
Cross section drawing of Sutton House by Georgina Allison

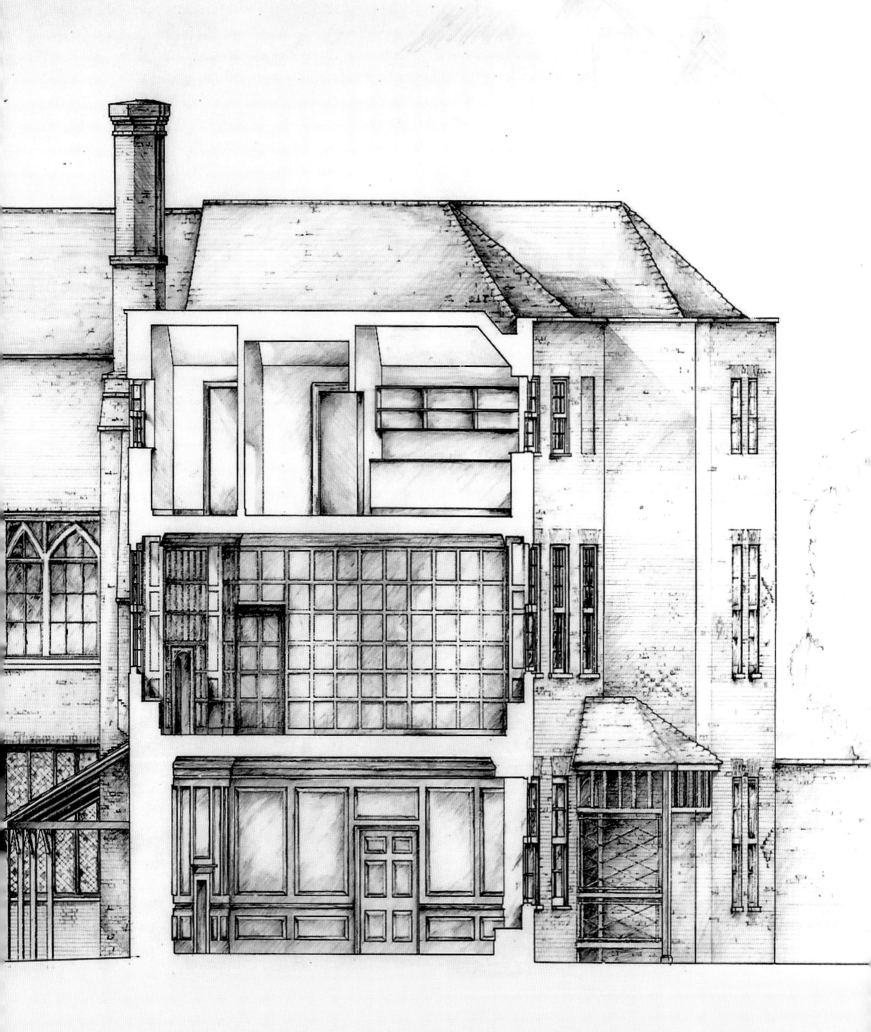

CHAPTER THREE

Old and new in context: Southwark Cathedral

For once, what one might call the Sackler Consensus – the dominant theory in conservation circles that all additions to historic buildings should be completely different from the original in style and material, like Norman Foster's Sackler Galleries at the Royal Academy – was ignored.
Giles Worsley, *The Daily Telegraph*, 30 June 2001: Southwark Cathedral, Romance in the stone

Three years after setting up Richard Griffiths Architects in 1993, my back bedroom was getting rather crowded, and I moved to Alan Baxter's workspace in Cowcross Street, home to many design professionals and amenity societies, especially those concerned with historic buildings. Alan Baxter and the historian Robert Thorne, proved marvellously supportive patrons, and helped me towards several of my early independent projects. I wanted to work on buildings in public rather than private ownership, and to this end applied for jobs as Cathedral Architect, a statutory appointment required of all Anglican Cathedrals. I was called for interview in 1996 at both Lincoln Cathedral and Southwark Cathedral, and had the daunting experience of visiting Lincoln with four fellow candidates for a low and high-level tour of the Cathedral and precinct, drinks and dinner with the Dean and Sub-Dean and members of the Chapter, followed by an interview the following morning. This was in the aftermath of the famous feud between the Dean and Sub-Dean following an (unsuccessful) fundraising visit with the Magna Carta to Australia, and I soon decided that I did not want the job after all.

Opposite
Southwark Cathedral
The new refectory and library uses the same palette of materials as the cathedral – stone and flint walls, copper roofs and oak joinery.

The interview at Southwark Cathedral followed shortly after, and they set an exercise – how to get visitors to donate money on entering or leaving the Cathedral. This was more like it, and I got on very well with Colin Slee, the wonderful, charismatic Dean, and with the members of the Fabric Advisory Committee, and was delighted to be appointed, despite having worked previously only for secular clients rather than for the Church. I had been greatly struck by the beauty of Southwark Cathedral and of its 20th century alterations on my first visit for a performance of Britten's Church Parable, the Prodigal Son, and looked forward to my work as Cathedral Architect. However, any leisure to gain an intimate knowledge of the Cathedral evaporated, three months into my appointment: the Cathedral's Millennium Project was longlisted in the last round of the Millennium Lottery, as one of three 'faith projects'. It was clear that the scheme on which the Millennium bid had been based would not obtain statutory consents. I was therefore asked to take responsibility for a £7m project designing a new entrance from the Thames Path, new buildings to house meeting rooms, refectory, library and shop, the conversion of the 1980's Chapter House, and the complete external cleaning and floodlighting of the Cathedral, together with substantial stone repairs.

We quickly came up with the concept of a new refectory wing at right angles to the Cathedral. This would enclose a three-sided new entrance courtyard, open towards the River Thames, having the scale of the monastic refectory and cloister destroyed after the Dissolution of the original Priory. The third side would be formed by a raised planting bed with a line of liquidamber trees, chosen for their scale and for their lovely red colour in Autumn. Fortunately, I had Ptolemy Dean, now Surveyor of Westminster Abbey, working with me. He shouldered the main load: dealing with the pressures of the timetable and the demands of the Millennium Lottery Fund, and in developing an appropriately contextual language for the relationship between the existing and the new buildings. The design that emerged from our discussions was a building made of the materials found in the Cathedral – stone with flint panels, copper roofs, mullioned and transomed windows and oak joinery – arranged in a manner related to precedent found elsewhere on Cathedral, while nevertheless being clearly contemporary. The internal structure is of paired beams of precast concrete and segmental vault sections on the ground floor, and of paired arched ribs of precast concrete, like cruck frames, to the library and meeting room that occupy the whole of the upper floor.

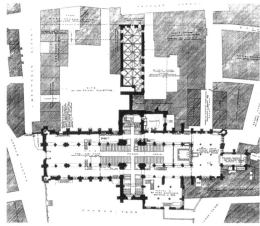

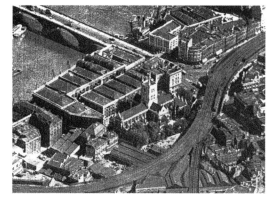

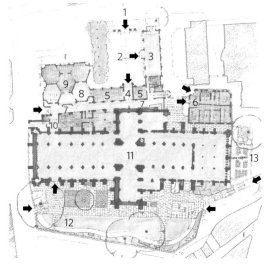

Top
The exterior of the new wing is built of Clipsham stone with knapped flint panels. The walls have insulated cavities around piers of brick on the ground floor and paired beams and ribs of pre-cast concrete on the upper floor.

Bottom left
ES Prior's wonderful Arts and Crafts church of St Andrew's, Roker, provided the inspiration for the ribs of the library.

Upper middle
The parish church of St Mary Overie in 1820 showing the surviving medieval refectory range.

Lower middle
The Cathedral in 1945 hemmed in by the railway to the south, London Bridge to the east and Hibernia Wharf to the north.

Bottom right
Southwark Cathedral plan.

Key
1   Thames path
2   Millennium courtyard
3   Refectory
4   North entrance
5   Meeting rooms
6   Cathedral offices
7   Link
8   Shop
9   Education
10 Cathedral entrance
11 Cathedral
12 South churchyard
13 Herb garden

Opposite
The library has paired ribs of pre-cast concrete that spring from floor level to support the oak roof. The oak bookcases have vestigial classical cornices.

Southwark Cathedral, whose buried 13th-century cloister will be revealed by building work costing £8 million. Worshippers have objected to the destruction of the chapter house, front, built ten years ago

£8m lottery demolition plan splits cathedral

Millennium project to create 'spiritual focus' at Southwark angers worshippers, reports Ruth Gledhill

Building is a political act, and the Millennium Project became mired in controversy. It had become clear to the Cathedrals Fabric Commission for England (who grant the ecclesiastical equivalent of listed building consent for work to Cathedrals) that the aim of making a historically appropriate new entrance from the river Thames could not be achieved if the office wing of the Chapter House, which lay on the axis of the transepts, were retained. We therefore embarked on a redesign with a new level, accessible and axial approach to the Cathedral via the Millennium Courtyard, leading to the north-west entrance via a shallowly sloping ramped and toplit passage between the Chapter House and the Victorian vestries, known as Launcelot's Link. There is another entrance to the Link at the west end, framed between the turret of the flint Chapter House and a new turret to the brick vestries, giving access to the roofs for maintenance. The east end of the Link leads to the Cathedral offices in Montague Chambers, thereby integrating them into the Cathedral precinct.

The destruction of the 1980's office wing gave occasion, for the only time in my life, for having my photograph published in the Times, holding a model of the new buildings under a headline that read *£8m lottery demolition plan splits Cathedral*. The previous Dean, who had commissioned the Chapter House, had launched a campaign to stop its demolition, and I was sent to visit him to explain why it could not be retained. Once I had done so, he said that, of course he could not agree with me, but he nevertheless thanked me for being the only person who had had the courtesy to visit and to attempt an explanation. After that, matters progressed more smoothly, except for the unexpected extent of the excavated archaeological remains of Roman roads and Norman and medieval fabric, which we managed to display publicly in an archaeological pit at the east end of the Link. Walter Lilly, our contractors, were happy to work on a historic building of national significance, and could not have been more helpful.

Ptolemy Dean and I were delighted that the Millennium Project won an RIBA and seven other design awards, and was shortlisted for the Accessibility Special Award at the RIBA Sterling Prize dinner at the Baltic Centre in Gateshead. We took the opportunity on the afternoon before the dinner to make a pilgrimage to ES Prior's church of St Andrew's, Roker, a locus classicus of the Arts and Crafts movement: this had provided the inspiration for the arched ribs of our library at Southwark Cathedral, like the ribcage of a great whale.

*Previous double page
Southwark Cathedral
began life as the medieval
Priory church of St Mary
Overie, became the parish
church of St Saviour's
Southwark after the
Dissolution, and became a
Cathedral in 1905. During
the Millennium project
the exterior was cleaned,
repaired and floodlit.*

*Top left
The end of Lancelot's
Link between the Chapter
House turret built by
my predecessor Ron
Sims and our new brick
turret extension to the
Victorian vestries. This
gives access to the roof for
maintenance.*

*Top right
Fame in the Times.*

*Opposite
Lancelot's Link contains
a gentle ramp leading up
from the new entrance
to the raised Chapter
House, then down to
the Cathedral via a
platform lift and steps. An
additional gable marks the
entrance to the Cathedral
between the existing
gables of the vestries.*

CHAPTER FOUR

Old and new in contrast: Lambeth Palace and Burghley House

New work should aspire to a quality of design and execution which may be valued both now and in the future. This neither implies nor precludes working in traditional or new ways, but should respect the significance of a place in its setting.

Historic England, *Conservation Principles*

Lambeth Palace is the London home of the Archbishop of Canterbury. It is the site of the decennial Lambeth Conference, of the Lambeth Palace Library and of offices of the Church of England. I received a letter one day asking if we wished to be considered for appointment for a project to create a new entrance for visitors, as the Palace was to be opened to the public for the first time as part of the Millennium 'String of Pearls'. The project had been devised by Richard Scott, one of the Scott dynasty and Palace Architect. It involved the creation of a new visitor entrance, the demolition of some post-War buildings by Seeley and Paget and the creation of a new courtyard covered with a glazed roof.   Accessible links between the entrance, the sunken courtyard, the crypt chapel and to the Guard Room on the upper floor would also be provided. We were delighted to be appointed to such an exciting project, not least because it offered the possibility to explore a language of contrast between old and new – and because we beat David Chipperfield.

Our new buildings at Southwark Cathedral had been designed in a contextual manner, using the palette of materials already present in the Cathedral. The design that Simon Ablett and I devised for the Lambeth Palace courtyard relied instead on a strong contrast between the heavyweight masonry walls of the medieval chapel and of Blore's Palace of the 1840's and the lightweight bronze-coated steel, glass and ash joinery of the roof and of the bridge that spans the courtyard. The latter is delicately detailed with doubled-up steel members with flitched connections. Similar detailing informs the balcony that overlooks the courtyard from above, and the glazed entrance screens to the new visitor entrance lobby. The courtyard was lowered to an intermediate level between entrance and crypt so as to reveal the sill of the medieval crypt window, but it transpired that Blore's foundations were in danger of being undermined. Our solution was to buttress the side of the walls with a reinforced concrete beam, clad in Ancaster stone, like the floor of the courtyard, so as to create a bench around the base of the courtyard walls, as often found in Renaissance palazzi in Italy. We have often found that an appeal to historical precedent can suggest appropriate solutions to practical or aesthetic problems.

Left
Lambeth Palace
The contrast of old and new in the courtyard.

In order to make all levels accessible, we inserted a lift adjacent to the courtyard in the only position possible to give access to ground, first and courtyard levels, with a separate platform lift adjacent to the steel, glass and timber steps leading down into the crypt chapel. You enter the platform lift from the landing via a hinged section of balustrade, and exit into the crypt chapel via a hinged glass panel. The lift is paved with floor tiles to match those in the Chapel, and when the lift is in the down position it is almost invisible. The lift and platform have been much illustrated in publications by Historic England as a model for the insertion of new design into an old building.

The glorious 13th-century crypt chapel (used by the Archbishop's household for their daily service) is furnished with the utmost simplicity, using solid ash for the altar and benches. These benches line the walls: they provide seating, but also cover the heating radiators and supply fixing points for electric sockets and lighting. The light shades are simple and cylindrical. They are set on the floor and illuminate the 13th-century ribbed vault from below. The crypt walls, which had been back-filled for centuries, were in poor condition, but we found that we could consolidate them successfully by raking out and repointing with a lime mortar. We did the same with the wall of the upper chapel facing the courtyard. The rich mix of materials – clunch, flint, stone, concrete and mortar – were left to tell the complicated archaeological story of alteration. Their varied ages, materials, textures and colours form a collage of great beauty.

At an early stage of the project we gave a presentation to Archbishop Carey, which, despite drawings, views and a model, elicited such an impassive response that I was surprised not to receive a letter terminating our appointment. Fortunately, it transpired that he was distracted by one of the crises that periodically afflict the Anglican Church, and we were delighted when he expressed his pleasure at the finished project. The project was shortlisted in the RFAC Building of the Year Awards, and we had a visitation by Lord St John of Fawsley and the other members of the assessment panel, all being filmed for television. After we had shown them around, Simon Ablett and I stood at the door while Lord St John drove off in his chauffeur-driven Daimler round the forecourt, his hand waving regally the whole way, his fellow judges following behind in a taxi.

Top left
The courtyard before demolition of Seeley and Paget's additions to reveal the elevations of the medieval chapel and Blore's 1840s palace.

Bottom left
The new courtyard was lowered to reveal the sill of the medieval window, with a perimeter seat faced with Ancaster stone.

Opposite
The 13th century crypt chapel is approached via steps and a barely visible platform lift, with a glazed door at crypt level and a gate in the balustrade at platform level.

Burghley House

A few years later, we were invited to submit competitive proposals for a new visitor project at Burghley House, the Elizabethan prodigy house outside Stamford in Lincolnshire. The project involved the conversion of Capability Brown's brewhouse into an introductory exhibition about the house and a display of some of its treasures, together with an extension in the rear courtyard between the Brewhouse and the stables. Simon Ablett and I adopted an approach that was similar to our previous work at Lambeth Palace, and designed the new building as a steel, glass and timber pavilion set in the Stamford stone courtyard. It shares one wall with the stables and its lovely oeil de boeuf windows. A separate tower (containing stairs and lift leading to the exhibition on the upper floor of the Brewhouse) is set in a narrow yard between the pavilion and the Brewhouse wall.

The pavilion was originally to have housed a collection of motor vehicles. However, it soon became clear that visitors would be highly unlikely to find their way to the Brewhouse, since the entrance to the house was on the opposite side. They would have been even less likely to visit the pavilion behind, at a dead end. We therefore suggested a radical solution: all visitors should enter via the pavilion instead, and buy tickets and orientate themselves there before passing through the upper and lower floors of the Brewhouse to view an introductory exhibition and a changing display of treasures from the collection. This works well, and the crisp contemporary detailing of the new entrance pavilion and stair tower, in oak, bronze-coated steel and glass, contrasts effectively with the weathered and decayed masonry and timber surfaces of the Brewhouse and stables. All visitors now enter our pavilion through an existing archway into a small paved yard, past a recumbent figure by Henry Moore, and thence proceed via the ticket desk and the Brewhouse to the house.

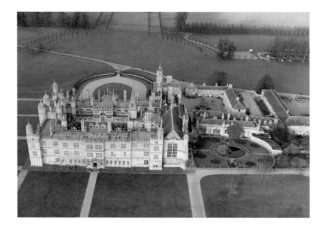

Previous double page
Lambeth Palace
The crypt chapel is heated by radiators fixed to the solid ash benches and lit by cylindrical bronze shades uplighting the vaults.

Top
Burghley House
The Elizabethan prodigy house: the Brewhouse courtyard to the right was the site for our new visitor building.

Bottom
The visitor entrance to the site is now through the archway to the new visitor building with ticketing, exhibition and education space.

Opposite
The new building is a pavilion of steel, glass and oak with a separate stair and lift tower giving access to the introductory exhibition on the first floor of the Brewhouse.

Top
One wall of the pavilion is formed by the stone wall and oeil-de-boeuf windows of the adjacent stable block.

Bottom left
The introductory exhibition on the first floor is effected by means of projection onto the walls. A changing exhibition of Burghley House treasures is displayed in showcases on the upper level.

Bottom right
A bronze figure by Henry
Moore sits adjacent to the
canopy in the entrance
courtyard.

CHAPTER FIVE

Historic houses for the public

A house was useful first and beautiful second. From this derives the joy of visiting English houses. They are a conversation between utility and beauty down the ages.
Simon Jenkins, *England's Thousand Best Houses*

We have been fortunate in working for the most part with historic houses maintained for the benefit of the public by local authorities, museums, the National Trust and English Heritage, rather than, like William Morris, 'ministering to the swinish luxury of the rich'. It is a great joy to be able to adapt historic houses to accommodate new uses, to see them being used and enjoyed by the public, and to give them a sustainable future. This is also, of course, the motivation of the National Lottery Heritage Fund (NLHF, formerly the HLF), and many of our projects have been carried out with their support. The project at Sutton House was a trail-blazer for the National Trust, working with the local community in the inner city. It received a Europa Nostra Award in recognition of its pioneering role in conservation and education. The project was also a trail-blazer in a different way. It was finished before the HLF was founded. Lord Rothschild (the first chairman of the HLF) referred in a lecture to the project at Sutton House as precisely the kind of project that the HLF was set up to support.

Eastbury Manor

Opposite
Eastbury Manor
The new oak staircase enclosure on the site of the collapsed Tudor stair turret.

We were early beneficiaries of HLF support at Eastbury Manor, a Tudor merchant's house of 1566 set implausibly in the middle of a 1930's housing estate in Barking. It is a wonderful H-shaped brick house built around a small courtyard with spiral stairs in each angle, one of which had collapsed in the early 19th century. The house had been preserved through the 19th century by virtue of its use as a farmhouse, stables and storage for farm vehicles, for which purpose large doorways had been cut through the walls. It was acquired in 1918 by the National Trust, working in association with the Society for the Protection of Ancient Buildings (SPAB), when the house was in danger of demolition as the rising tide of London development approached Barking. The architectural interest and importance of the house had been recognised in a book published as early as the 1840's, and again in an early 1911 monograph published by the Survey of London. This was set up by CR Ashbee in 1900 to record and to make the case for the preservation of historic buildings at risk, many of them in East London. Ashbee is one of my heroes, architect of the lovely free-school houses in Cheyne Walk, exquisite silversmith and founder of the Guild of Handicraft (while a volunteer at Toynbee Hall, another of our projects).

Eastbury Manor was repaired in 1935 by William Weir, the pre-eminent SPAB architect (this did not prevent him restoring the Tudor house by infilling the carthouse openings). It was converted to house the short-lived Barking Museum which closed during WWII in 1940. When I was first engaged to carry out a Quinquennial Survey for the National Trust in 1989, the house was in the hands of the Barking Arts Trust, each club or society having its own room with its own locked door. Later, however, the Council decided to take the house back under its direct control, and appointed a wonderful curator, Cherry Buckley, who began putting on activities and events for local people – including very popular murder mystery evenings – and it became the preferred location for meetings, conferences and training sessions for the Council itself. The whole house started to buzz with life, despite the primitive accommodation.

The first step in the transformation of the house was a project paid for entirely by the Council, renewing the antiquated electrics and removing some of the modern partitions. By this stage, I was working as architect for the Council, and prepared a Conservation and Development Plan for the house. At the same time Marylla Hunt of Landscape Design Associates prepared a Conservation and Development Plan for the grounds. In the process she discovered a 1737 plan of the house in its wider setting. Our plan was implemented in two phases. The first phase concerned the west wing of the house. We made it fully accessible by means of external ramps and the insertion of a platform lift, and converted it to provide reception, café, shop, meeting rooms, education room and administration office. The café is sited in the Tudor kitchen, and is linked by means of an external ramp screened by a dwarf wall and planting to a new kitchen garden inspired by the layout shown on the 1737 plan.

A few years after the successful completion of the first phase, Eastbury Manor was awarded a further HLF grant to implement the second phase.

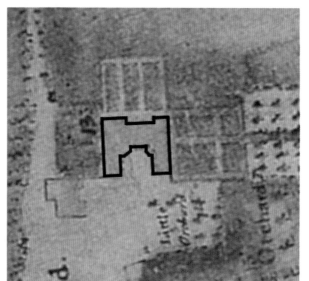

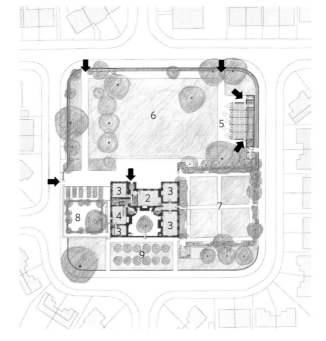

Previous double page
Eastbury Manor *is an H-shaped Tudor house of c1566 arranged around a south-facing courtyard. One of the two stair turrets in the angles collapsed in the early 19th century, and we replaced it with a steel spiral staircase within a new oak-boarded enclosure.*

Top
Eastbury Manor as a farmhouse in 1833.

Middle
1737 map of the grounds showing parterres to west and north, and an avenue of tress extending from the walled garden to the east.

Bottom
Site plan of Eastbury Manor showing the proposed new café in a re-landscaped setting.

Key
1   Entrance/lift
2   Tudor hall
3   Parlours
4   Tudor kitchen
5   Cafe
6   Front lawn
7   Walled garden
8   Kitchen garden
9   Orchard

Top
The fire compartmentation screen in the attic is constructed of oak to match the exposed Tudor roof timbers.

Middle left
The Tudor stair is made of solid oak tress, housed into a central oak port that runs full-height.

Middle right
The new stair follows the geometry of the lost Tudor stair, albeit in the reverse direction, with oak treads fixed to the steel treads.

Bottom right
The surviving Tudor stair is still used for access and means of escape, for which purpose we fitted an iron handrail with cobra-headed finials.

This completed the repair and re-servicing of the central hall range and east wing, provided fire compartmentation in the attics, and enclosed the ruined east staircase around a new spiral stair. The oak framed and boarded enclosure followed the original geometry in a contemporary manner. This proved controversial with some members of the National Trust Architectural Panel who wanted a full restoration of the collapsed east stair turret to match the surviving Tudor west stair turret. I thought that the remains of the turret, already shown as a ruin in the print of 1833, were significant in their own right, and proposed a rustic enclosure of oak framing and flush oak boarding, appropriate to the 19th century farmhouse. The great cost of a full restoration proved prohibitive, and the oak stair turret was built.

A third HLF project is now being planned to improve the walled garden and to address the wider issue of how the grounds can be improved to provide an amenity for local residents and visitors, and a setting for large events. This bears witness to the transformation of Eastbury Manor from 'a bottomless pit of wasted expenditure' to 'the jewel in the heritage of Barking'.

Clissold House

Our experience at Sutton House and at Eastbury Manor proved vital when we carried out the HLF-funded project at Clissold House, a fine late Georgian villa in Stoke Newington, at the heart of one of the loveliest and most heavily used public parks in London. I had lived in the area since moving to London in 1986, and the café at Clissold House had always been a central part of Stoke Newington life, albeit rather shabbily taking up the main reception rooms. The café was cut off from the rest of the house, which was largely derelict, and its kitchen was situated in the original library, the extractor fan blowing out through one of its windows. The house had suffered a fire and was largely derelict, the roof was leaking, there were outbreaks of dry rot, and the lower ground floor had been largely destroyed by a former conversion to sports changing rooms. The project aimed to restore the derelict house and to make it fully accessible as an improved public café and venue for functions and events on the upper floors. It had received HLF funding as part of the overall renewal of Clissold Park, and we were appointed to see the works on the house through to completion.

It was clear to me, as a longstanding local resident, that there was a fundamental conflict between the significance of the architecture of the house and the significance of its use as a café, a vital feature in the life of Stoke Newington. Early prints and photographs of the house show its appearance as a temple sitting atop a grassy knoll in an Arcadian landscape overlooking a bend of the New River, its remarkable early Greek (rather than Roman) Doric columns standing on a stepped stylobate without bases. Yet the café and its kitchen occupied the main historic rooms of the house, and the slope of the grassy knoll had been levelled to a muddy terrace covered with plastic tables. Our solution was to create a second external terrace for the café at the lower level. This was adjacent to the relocated kitchen in the vaulted undercroft and overlooked the

Previous double page
Clissold House *was designed in 1790, probably by Daniel Alexander, and restored with HLF funding in 2013.*

Top
Clissold House in 1876, a Grecian villa set in an Arcadian landscape atop a grassy knoll.

Middle
The front lawn before the work, a muddy patch of grass with ugly walls.

Bottom
The function room before work started.

Top left
The restored staircase seen
from the upper ground
floor corridor.

Top right
The entrance hall was
re-opened to the staircase,
which had previously been
hidden from public view.

Right
Lower ground, upper
ground and first floor plans
following the work.

Key
1   Park WC's
2   Accessible entrance
3   Lift
4   Staircase
5   House WC's
6   Kitchen
7   Back of House
8   South terrace
9   West terrace
10   Cafe servery
11   Cafe
12   Function room

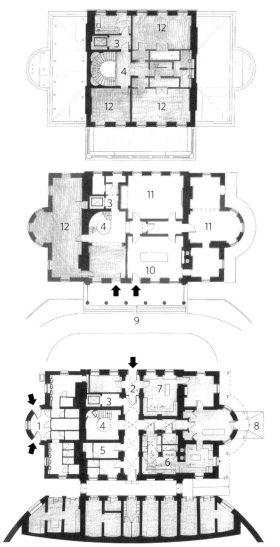

restored pleasure garden to the south. Linking the two levels of the café and the kitchen by means of a pair of dumb waiters required the complete removal of the brick chimney breasts on two levels and the re-supporting of the chimneys on large steels, now hidden by the rebuilt original wall profile on both sides.

We had more difficulty with the removal of the terrace facing the New River to restore the grass slope. We had been careful to demonstrate that the scale and outlook of the external seating that could be provided on the new south terrace would more than compensate for the loss of seating on the grass slope. This did not, however, prevent the launch of a local petition called, inappropriately, 'Save Our Slope'. Fortunately, the Clissold Park Users Group backed our proposal, and the historic slope was restored. When I pass the house in summer I am always delighted to see so many people enjoying the park and the café, eating out on the south lawn and under the Doric colonnade, or sitting on the sloping lawn in front of the house and enjoying the idyllic view over the New River.

CHAPTER SIX

The care of churches

It is possible to come across the perfect village church quite by chance, breaking a journey on impulse, entering without premeditation to receive some of the most exquisite pleasure that building can offer.
Edwin Smith, Graham Hutton and Olive Cook, *English Parish Churches,* 1976

To the incumbent the church is a workshop; to the antiquary it is a relic. To the parish it is a utility; to the outsider a luxury. How do we unite these incompatibles?
Thomas Hardy, *Memories of Church Restoration,* 1906

Working with churches is fundamentally different from working with secular buildings. When the statutory system for obtaining consent for alterations to listed buildings was first established in 1949, the Church of England opted out on the grounds that it already had its own internal controls under the Faculty system, established under ecclesiastical rather than secular law. In the case of churches, consent has to be obtained from the Diocesan Advisory Committee (DAC) and from the Chancellor of the Diocese, and in the case of Cathedrals from the Cathedral's Fabric Advisory Committee (FAC) or, in major cases, from the Cathedrals Fabric Commission for England (CFCE). The FAC's and DAC's have a panel of experts, some in history or conservation, some in liturgical matters. They make the delicate judgements between considerations of the church's historic fabric and considerations of the church's present-day needs, expressed in a Statement of Need.

Opposite
**St Nicholas' Chapel
Kings Lynn**
View of the nave from the inside of the tower.

When I began my career, no such distinction existed in controls to secular listed buildings. The preservation of historic fabric took precedence over considerations of reuse and sustainability. Conservation philosophy still derived from Ruskin – 'we have no right whatever to touch them' – and from the SPAB – 'put Protection in place of Restoration'. This way of thinking has now been superseded, thanks to the NLHF who needed a more sophisticated way of assessing applications. They adopted the methodology of the Conservation Plan, ironically first developed in Australia by James Semple Kerr in 1982. The steps of the Conservation Plan process are to understand the history of the building or place, to assess its significance, to investigate the issues facing it and to devise appropriate policies to sustain its future. The impact of the proposals on that significance can then be assessed. It is the balancing of need and intervention, and the adding of new fabric to old in buildings of great age and beauty, that makes working with old buildings so challenging and rewarding.

St Alfege, Greenwich

I was invited in 1996 to interview for the position of church architect at St Alfege, Hawksmoor's great church in Greenwich, designed in 1721, and asked how I would provide equal access to the floor of the church, which is seven steps higher than the external ground level on all sides. In view of the difficulty of integrating the design of a ramp or lift into Hawksmoor's noble architecture (the church is described in his published print as a Templum, or Roman temple), I proposed a gently curving external ramp and bridge of lightweight stainless steel and timber, contrasting with Hawksmoor's heavy masonry, leading to the south entrance of the church. We are finally, twenty years later, about to install such a ramp (albeit on the north side of the church facing the Maritime Greenwich World Heritage Site) as part of a project to open the church more widely to the public, to replace the leaking roofs, to complete the cleaning of the Portland stone elevations and

to open the crypt to the public for hard hat tours. Since the crypt, still full of burials, will not be accessible to all, a 3D laser point cloud has been produced for download from the church website, depicting church and crypt with a ghost-like appearance for all to access.

The project, funded by the NLHF, is a fine example of the transformation that can be achieved to make historic buildings accessible to the public, and to give them a more sustainable future. It also illustrates how the historic research that is integral to the Conservation Plan process can lead to new understanding of the building and its architectural intentions. During the course of the historical research, a previously unidentified drawing was found in the Greenwich archive collection that has now been confirmed as being in Hawksmoor's own hand. The drawing sheds new light on the relationship between Hawksmoor's design for the church and his intentions for rebuilding the medieval tower.

Top
St Alfege, Greenwich, *was Hawksmoor's first independent commission in 1721. The medieval tower was later refaced by John James. We cleaned and repaired the stonework of the tower, removing the rusting iron cramps and lighting the elevation.*

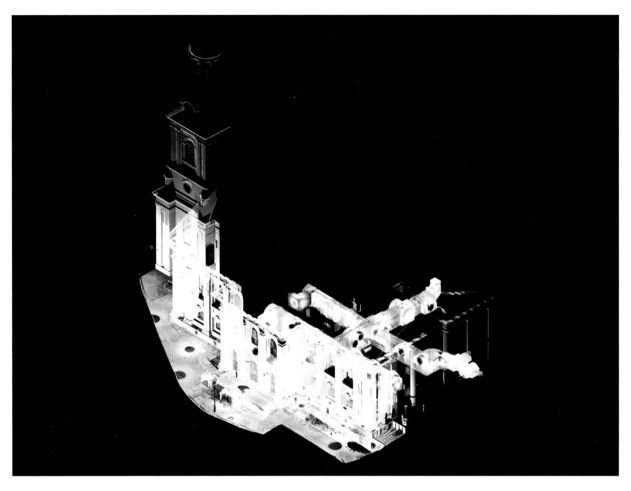

St Alfege is widely used for concerts by the Tallis Choir and by the Trinity College of Music, which is based at the Royal Naval College. This is typical of the extended range of uses to which church buildings are increasingly put, nowhere more so than by the Churches Conservation Trust, owner of 350 churches no longer required for regular worship. I was a Trustee during the period that saw the transformation of a body set up to preserve redundant churches to one focused on conserving churches and providing the widest possible access to them. The Trust is best known for saving the derelict Georgian church of St Paul's, Bristol, in the then notorious St Paul's area of Bristol. I feel a sense of vicarious satisfaction since I recommended the contact who identified Circomedia, a circus training school, as the ideal tenant. An aerial rig has been hung from the roof structure via small (and therefore reversible) holes drilled in the elaborate plaster ceiling, from which aerial acrobatics can be carried out in blissful counterpoint to the architecture.

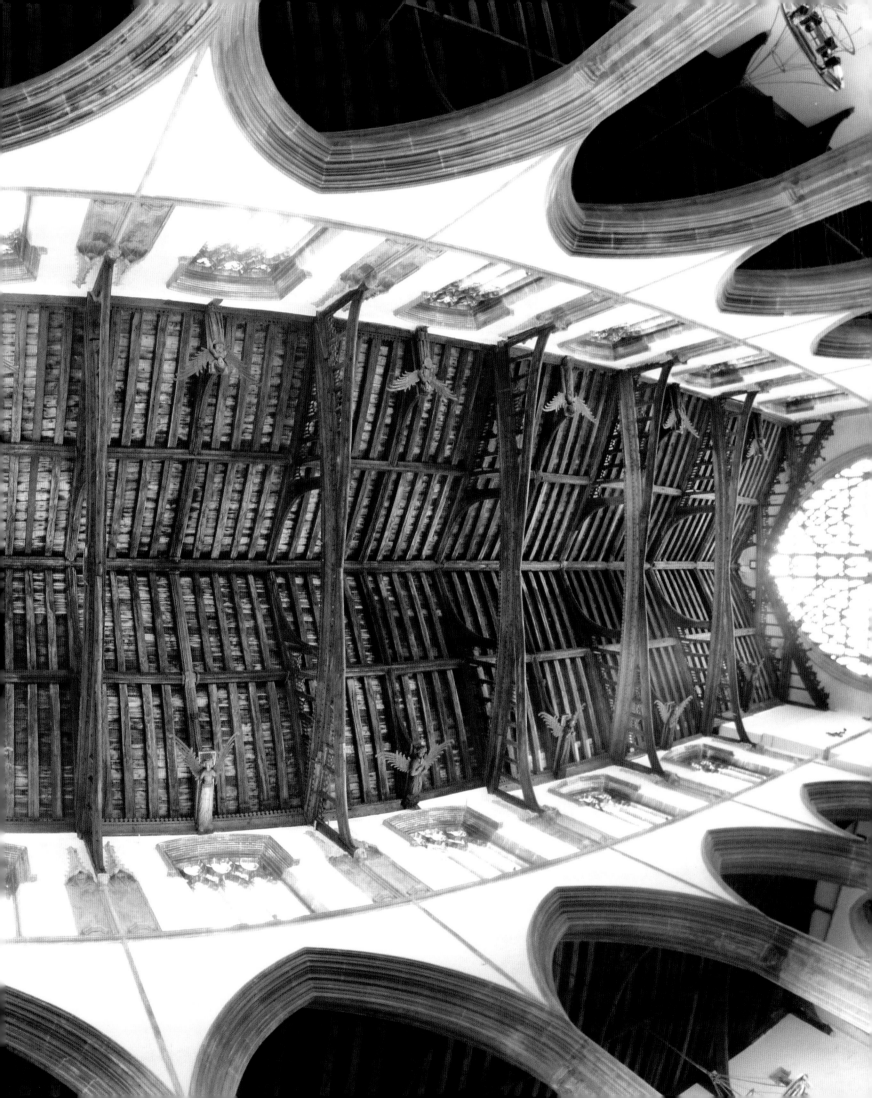

St Nicholas' Chapel, King's Lynn

Our most notable project for the CCT was the NLHF-funded project at St Nicholas' Chapel, King's Lynn. This was formerly a chapel of ease to the parish church, albeit a vast building and the largest chapel in England. It is a magnificent and little altered testament to the quality of 15th-century Gothic and to the maritime wealth of the merchants of King's Lynn. It has rich timberwork and the lovely carved angles on the trusses of the nave roof bear traces of their original painted decoration. Like much of our work involving historic houses, this project was funded by the HLF. We had to repair the fabric, including complete re-roofing with lead, to install interpretation panels and to provide facilities for

other uses, especially large concerts as part of the King's Lynn Festival. We shoe-horned toilets, kitchen and access for the bellringers into the constricted space of the tower, and additional toilets into the base of the tower, accessed from outside for use during major events. The most notable aspect of our work was the approach to heating. The chapel is long and tall, there is no gas supply, and the cost of heating the church to comfort conditions, or anything remotely resembling them, would have been so high as to be unsustainable. We therefore successfully made the case for the installation of electric radiant heaters to the nave, powered by the largest array of photo-voltaic panels installed at that date in any church in the country, occupying the full length of the south nave roof slope. The church had been lit previously by chandeliers in the nave arcades in two tiers, looking like lobster pots. We adapted the design to accommodate two circular metal bands supporting a hexagonal array of small radiant heaters, pendant lights and uplighters. The installation is sustainable economically, environmentally and indeed socially, thanks to the greater use to which the chapel can now be put, and to the place that it holds in the hearts and minds of the people of King's Lynn and of visitors from afar.

Previous double page
St Nicholas Chapel, King's Lynn*, was repaired and adapted for a wide range of public uses for the Churches Conservation Trust. The project conserved the remarkable medieval roof with its carved angels and extensive surviving medieval decoration.*

Top
The nave is heated and lit by means of chandeliers inspired by the existing 'lobsterpot' chandeliers, with a ring of infra-red heaters and two rings of pendant lights.

Left
The roof was entirely relaid with new cast lead supporting a large array of photovoltaic panels.

St Mary's, Twickenham

Our project at St Mary's, Twickenham was designed to provide a strong architectural and theological rationale for its reordering and for the removal of the Victorian pews. The church was designed by John James in the early 18th century. It is remarkable both for the exaggerated scale of its Doric gallery fronts, and for its strong cross axis, like a Greek Cross in plan, a feature that it shares with contemporary churches by Wren, Hawksmoor and Thomas Archer. We proposed three new points of focus on the axis of the Greek Cross: a new altar to the east, a lectern to the west and a candle in the centre, as a sign of peace and hope. This threefold focus was also intended to symbolise the Trinity. Around these points of focus new oak benches would be arranged in collegiate manner for services, facing inwards, or re-arranged facing eastwards for concerts or large services. The floor would be relaid with stone flags, incorporating the existing ledger stones and three new inscribed stones below the three points of liturgical focus. The threefold focus would also be marked by three large Dutch chandeliers hanging from new ceiling roses.

The first phase has been completed, with the removal of the choir stalls and the installation of an accessible platform paved with Belgian black and Carrara white marble tiles. Other phases will follow, subject to successful fundraising.

Top
St Mary's Church, Twickenham *Long section of the re-ordered church.*

Upper right
The choir platform cleared of choirstalls and laid with a geometric floor pattern of white Carrara and black Belgian marble tiles.

Middle right
The plan of the church before work started.

Bottom right
The masterplan for re-ordering the whole church and extending the galleries is arranged around triple foci of altar, lectern and candle, symbolising God, Christ as the incarnate Word, and the Holy Spirit

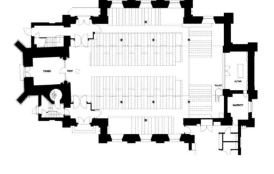

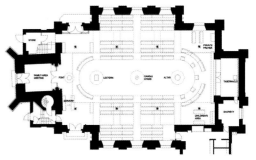

Methodist Central Hall

Methodist Central Hall is the headquarters of the Methodist Church, combining religious, public and administrative functions. It was designed in an extravagant Edwardian Baroque style by Lanchester and Rickards in 1909, with a grand oval entrance hall and staircase leading to the Great Hall on the second floor. The Hall is used extensively for conferences, (including the Inaugural General Assembly of the United Nations in 1946), choral concerts and public inquiries, as well as for church services. Simon Ablett, then an Associate, was appointed architect in 2000, and oversaw a major programme of repairs and upgrading.

The major issue was the lack of adequate access to the Hall for visitors with disabilities, and the lack of flexibility for adapting the Hall to its different uses. The problems of access were finally solved by creating a new entrance for the disabled adjacent to a new double lift shaft linking spaces at all levels of the building. The shaft was formed by the removal on one whole staircase of the two identical stairs flanking the Baroque main staircase; we could do this without loss of fire escape capacity by upgrading and bringing into public use a secondary service stair. This left the problem of access between the floor of the Great Hall, the platform, and the raked seating for the choir. We had the idea of extending the existing platform with an oval extension, appropriate to a building in the Edwardian Baroque. This was designed in five sections which can be easily raised and lowered independently, by means of five scissor lifts, between the platform level, one step height above floor level for communion, and the floor level of the Hall. The central section can even be lowered to the level of a redundant air duct below the floor, and used for storing the grand piano when not in use. Thanks to the oval platform and the scissor lifts the Hall can be easily rearranged between a morning service and an evening concert.

Opposite
Methodist Central Hall
The new oval platform, appropriate to Lanchester's Edwardian Baroque, can be easily reconfigured to allow for communion services at the weekend and conferences and concerts during the week.

Top
The new lift core contains two lifts and an air shaft occupying the former stair enclosure.

Middle left
The lift core was formed by removing one of two identical stairs leading to the third floor Great Hall.

Bottom left
The platform is configured as five independent scissor lifts that allow a variety of heights to suit different stage layouts, for different uses.

CHAPTER SEVEN

The care of cathedrals: St Albans Abbey

The presence in our midst of these extraordinary buildings, rooted in the past and embodying ideals and aspirations so different from our own, is the source of a reassuring sense of continuity. But changes, revolutionary changes, since the time of the Reformation, have been taking place in the fabric and liturgical arrangement of the cathedrals throughout the centuries.
Edwin Smith and Olive Cook, *English Cathedrals,* 1989

By ecclesiastical law, every cathedral has to have a Cathedral Architect, a position equivalent to the role of Surveyor to the Fabric that Sir Christopher Wren held at St Paul's Cathedral. The best possible epitaph for an architect was written on his tomb: *si monumentum requiris, circumspice* (If you seek his monument, look around you). In 2000, as the Millennium project at Southwark Cathedral reached completion, I was appointed Cathedral Architect at St Albans Abbey, and began a surveyorship that lasted 18 years. It was a wonderful position to have, a 'friend of the cathedral' with responsibility for the fabric and the architectural integrity of the building, its repair and its alteration to suit the changing pattern of liturgy, new needs and extended uses. In this context, it is vital for the Cathedral Architect to keep in mind a long-term vision for change in the cathedral, maintaining its integrity while repairing it to reveal the beauty of the past, and adapting it to meet the requirements of the present and of the future. The pressures in a Cathedral on the Dean and Chapter are primarily liturgical, practical and economic rather than architectural, and the Cathedral Architect's duty is to steer a course between Scylla and Charybdis, the needs of the old and the needs of the new.

I spent my first few months at St Albans reining in some projects already in preparation that were motivated by the availability of funding, but that appeared to me inappropriate. I needed to ensure that projects fitted within an overall vision for the development of the Cathedral, and feared that my appointment might be abruptly terminated. I survived, and reached an agreement, with the support of the FAC, that before embarking on any project I should be commissioned to provide a masterplan for the future potential development of at least that part of the Cathedral to which the project related. During my time as Cathedral Architect I completed 35 projects over 17 years, an average of two projects a year. The masterplan provided a vital overview, ensuring that the cumulative effect of all the projects exceeded the sum of their parts. This was recognised by the RIBA National Award in 2017 in accepting our work as a single project lasting 18 years. The achievement was made possible by my assistants John Woodcock then Kathryn Harris, who oversaw the execution of a programme of work of great complexity and refinement.

At the beginning, I completed some conservation projects already in progress, including the conservation of the medieval ceiling and the wall paintings, each realised over the course of six or seven annual phases of work. It was the access project that first allowed me to consider the Cathedral as a whole.

Opposite
St Albans Abbey
The planes of recession of the Norman arches at St Albans are based on the module of the reused Roman bricks.

The 22 steps between the entrance doors to the west and the shrine chapel to the east constituted a barrier to disabled visitors more serious than that at any other cathedral. The strategy that I prepared has now been realised by the creation of an accessible processional route leading from the west end to the Lady Chapel at the east, and thence to the St Alban shrine chapel behind the High Altar. A new paved forecourt outside the west front leads the full length of the cathedral via steps, ramps and platform lifts that divide the width of the aisles in two. At the east end the route leads finally to the shrine of St Alban via new processional steps, flanked by walls screening steps for the ambulant disabled to the south and a platform lift to the north.

The exterior improvements effected during my time as Cathedral Architect included the conservation of medieval stonework in the eastern parts of the Cathedral and in the remains of the monastic cloister. We also cleaned, conserved and gave a lime shelter coating to the medieval west porches, one of the finest architectural features of the Abbey, and painted the west doors red following medieval precedent.

Inside the Abbey, the main intervention was the cleaning, repair and limewashing of the early Norman nave, one of the most impressive architectural features of the Abbey with its primitive planes of recession derived from the size of the Roman bricks with which it is built. In the repaired nave we introduced a new nave sanctuary three bays long with a complete new set of nave furniture. This was designed in conjunction with Luke Hughes, who also refitted the area under the organ as part of the processional route, flanked by storage cupboards carefully designed to store all the choir furniture and staging. This allows the flexible use of the nave platform for every scale of event, up to the large choral and orchestral concerts for which the Abbey is so well suited.

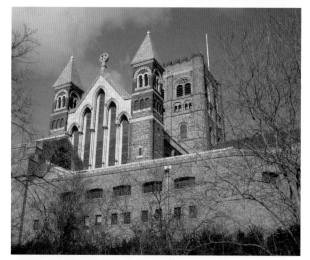

Top
St Albans Abbey
One of the most significant survivals of the medieval Abbey is that of the cloister remains built into the south wall of the nave. We cleaned, conserved and protected the soft clunch stonework with a lime shelter-coat, and provided overhanging lead caps to the broken springing of the vaults, the tas-de-charge.

Upper left
The cloister remains before repair and conservation.

Lower left
St Albans Abbey seen from the south with its three layers of architectural history. The early Norman Tower was built of bricks salvaged from the Roman town of Verulamium at the bottom of the hill; the south transept was refaced by Lord Grimthorpe in the 1870's; and the Chapter House was added by William Whitfield in the 1980's.

Bottom left
A dramatic view of the Cathedral seen from the east.

Top left
We cleaned and conserved the west porches, architecturally perhaps the finest feature of the Abbey. These were only completed in the 1870's by Lord Grimthorpe. Not known for modesty, he represented himself as the Evangelist Matthew in the main entrance.

Top right
The oak doors were painted red to enliven the porch according to medieval precedent.

Bottom right
The new enlarged nave sanctuary seen from the west flanked by the Norman and Gothic arcades, with new nave platform, choir furniture, altar and new sculpted figures on the medieval pulpitum screen by Rory Young. The new choir stalls are divided to allow the processional axis to extend to the full length of the cathedral.

From the nave, the processional route passes under the organ and emerges into the choir which is used mainly for evensong, that unique creation of the Anglican Church. The Master of Music had been given a legacy for the enlargement of the choir stalls to accommodate the whole choir. The only way to achieve this was to shorten the middle bank of stalls by one stall, to extend the choir stalls by adding the removed stall, and to relocate the steps in between, an operation that might sound simple but in fact proved highly complicated. With the addition of new reading shelves, candle lights and architectural lighting, the stalls have been transformed; yet it is the fate of the Cathedral Architect that visitors assume that what they see has always been like that, and do not appreciate the intervention unless it is explained to them.

The processional route proceeds past the high altar screen with its extraordinary reredos by

Top
View to the high altar through the doorway leading into the choir below the organ gallery.

Bottom
The stalls in the quire are in three groups. In order to accommodate the complete choir we extended the choir stalls by moving one stall from the middle group, a delicate and almost invisible operation. We also provided new bronze lecterns and oil candle lights with glass shades.

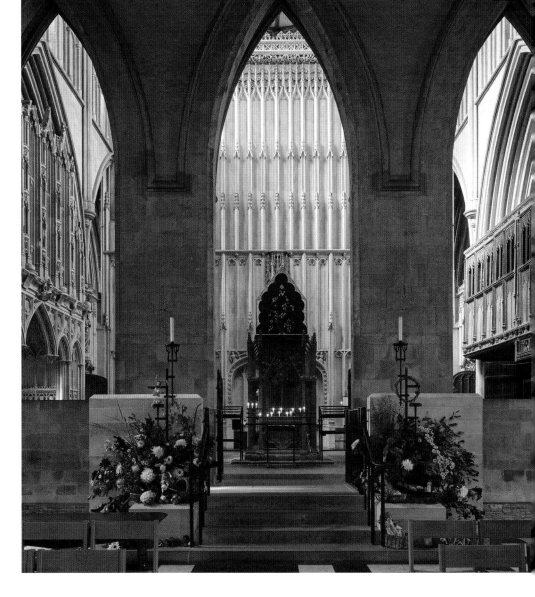

Alfred Gilbert, the sculptor of Eros in Piccadilly Circus. It leads via the ambulatories to the Lady Chapel at the east end of the Cathedral, the extremely dirty walls of which we successfully cleaned by means of the same latex technique used at St Paul's Cathedral. Ascending our new steps and platform lift, the processional route finally turns to terminate at the shrine of St Alban, the Roman soldier who gave shelter to a Christian during the persecutions of the Emperor Diocletian, was martyred and became the first English saint. The early Norman Abbey was built on the site of his martyrdom, appropriately using bricks salvaged from the Roman city of Verulamium at the bottom of the hill. The shrine, destroyed at the Dissolution, was rediscovered by Sir George Gilbert Scott and reconstructed in recent years. It is once again the destination of the processional route, as it was for the medieval pilgrims, overseen from the extraordinary medieval watching loft.

Top right
The new platform and flanking walls complete the processional axis that runs the full length of the Abbey, culminating in the shrine of St Alban at the highest point of the Abbey.

Bottom left
The steps to the shrine chapel before alteration. The seats formed part of the consistory court designed by Lord Grimthorpe following the removal of the passageway through the (then) parish church.

Bottom right
The new platform is flanked by steps for the ambulant disabled and a platform lift concealed by screen walls, allowing access for all.

Right
The brief for the new window by Caroline Benyon was for figures of the Virgin and St Columba in arched architectural frames, as found in the adjacent Victorian windows. She has realised this in an extraordinary way, the frame and figures blending together with a wealth of detail realised using coloured glass inherited from Christopher Whall.

Not least of the responsibilities of the Cathedral Architect is in helping to ensure that works designed to form part of the permanent fabric are worthy and can stand the test of time. I was involved in the commissioning of a new nave stained glass window representing St Mary and St Columba by Caroline Benyon. She devised an interesting variant on the tradition of representing saints in architectural frames, as found in the adjacent 19th century stained glass windows.

She belongs in the arts and crafts tradition in a direct line from Christopher Whall, whose collection of coloured glass she inherited. The design, as well as the glass and the leading is full of interest and of inventive detail derived from the story of the saint. I also researched possible sculptors for a set of seven statues of modern martyrs to be installed in the pulpitum screen above the nave altar, leading to the appointment of Rory Young.

One project remains unexecuted, the Great Tower Project to rehang a new peal of 13 bells within a new lantern at the top of the tower. The sightlines between the ringers in the ringing stage of the tower were poor because of the obstruction caused by large raking axial medieval timbers, which caused the ringing circle to be placed in one quarter of the area of the ringing chamber. We planned to move the ringers up to the bell stage with unobstructed sightlines, and to create a new radial ring of 13 bells on a concrete platform at the top of the tower, supported by raking steel legs designed to return the load of the bells to the same level as before. The platform was to be penetrated by holes for the ropes that reflected the size of the bells above. In order to construct the new peal of bells it was necessary

to remove the roof structure designed by Lord Grimthorpe who rebuilt much of the Abbey in the 1860's at his own expense and whose insensitivity appalled William Morris and the SPAB. We proposed a new octagonal oak roof structure based on the medieval predecessor illustrated by Neale in his great book recording the Abbey before its restoration. The new ring of bells would have been an extraordinary intervention in the Norman tower; however, it proved impossible to fund, and a new peal has now been fitted at the existing level, improving the operation of the bells, if not the sightlines of the bellringers. The extraordinary Great Tower Project is nevertheless memorialised in the splendid 3D cut-away view by the engineers, Price and Myers.

Top
The Great Tower project was for the rehanging of a radial peal of bells on a concrete platform at the top of the tower, supported on raking steel legs that would have allowed clear sightlines for all the ringers. The 3D rendering records how it would have appeared.

CHAPTER EIGHT

New design in historic contexts

I once had an intern student from the eminent Waterloo School of Architecture in Canada, who said of the practice *You know, RGA is so retro it is almost avant-garde!* I took this as a compliment, that an approach to architecture inspired by works of all periods and by its historic context, and using materials in their natural state, could be resolutely forward-looking in intent, and indifferent to fashion. In my view, true sustainability lies in the creation of buildings with a low carbon footprint, using natural materials and designed flexibly for the long term on the principle of long life, loose fit.

St Paul's Hammersmith

Opposite
St Paul's Hammersmith
The interior of the atrium opens to the former baptistery of the church through three sets of glazed oak doors.

Bottom left
Old St Peter's in 6th century Rome had a western atrium that inspired our atrium at St Paul's.

Bottom right
The plan of St Paul's Hammersmith with its western atrium.

St Paul's Hammersmith, the tall Gothic church by the one-way system next to the Hammersmith flyover, was taken over in the 1990's by an evangelical congregational plant from Holy Trinity Brompton. Since then, it has expanded rapidly with a growing congregation and an extraordinarily wide social mission embracing debt counselling, night shelter, courses, concerts and much more. The search for space to accommodate the 17 people working at the church had led to unsuccessful projects to build a new building between the church and the flyover, and a large gallery within the church. We were appointed because we told the church that we thought we could obtain consent for a new

building at the west end of the church, a more prominent, and therefore sensitive, position. Our confidence was based on the precedent of the early Christian tradition of the western atrium, as found in the first St Peter's in Rome, with ranges of buildings around a courtyard facing the west end of the church. In early Christian examples, the courtyard was open and symbolised a Paradise garden, but in our proposal the central atrium covered the assembly hall, with three sets of double doors linking to the western apse of the church and two of the tallest doors in London, allowing the west doors of our extension to be thrown open in summer to embrace the green outside.

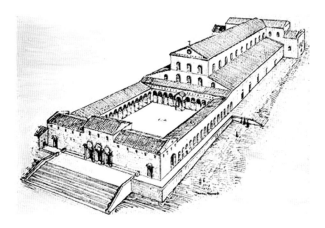

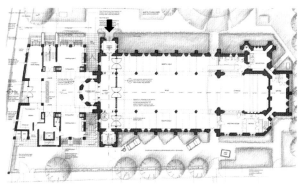

Old St Peter's may have provided an appropriate historical reference, but it was not sufficient to relate the new building to its present day context. In the first scheme, this was achieved by retaining the oblique brick wall marking the limit of the historic churchyard, with a floating upper floor inspired by Le Corbusier's Villa Savoye. This proved too much for the Hammersmith and Fulham Society, and the design team led by Malcom Fryer redesigned the building with the assembly hall on the line of the nave, flanking buildings on the line of the aisles, and balconies overlooking the Green on the line of the porches. This provides a richly varied composition of forms, materials and textures: roofs of copper, sedum and copper, walls of ashlar stonework,

windows with bronze frames and doors of oak. The Bath stone of our new building matches the quoins (corner stones) of the Victorian church, rather than its walls of pink sandstone. It thereby relates to the church without competing with it.

The church was determined that the new building should be welcoming and inclusive, despite its position in the centre of the Hammersmith gyratory. The balconies facing west overlook the north churchyard, which is in turn overlooked from the Broadway, and the glazed oak doors provide welcome during the day and a beacon at night to café, bookshop, classes, meetings and courses available to the whole community.

Top
The interior of the atrium acts as an assembly hall with bookshop, café and meeting rooms.

Opposite
The extension seen through the doors from the baptistery of the church, now redecorated in strong medieval-inspired colours.

Double page over
The great west doors and the balconies act as a beacon after dark.

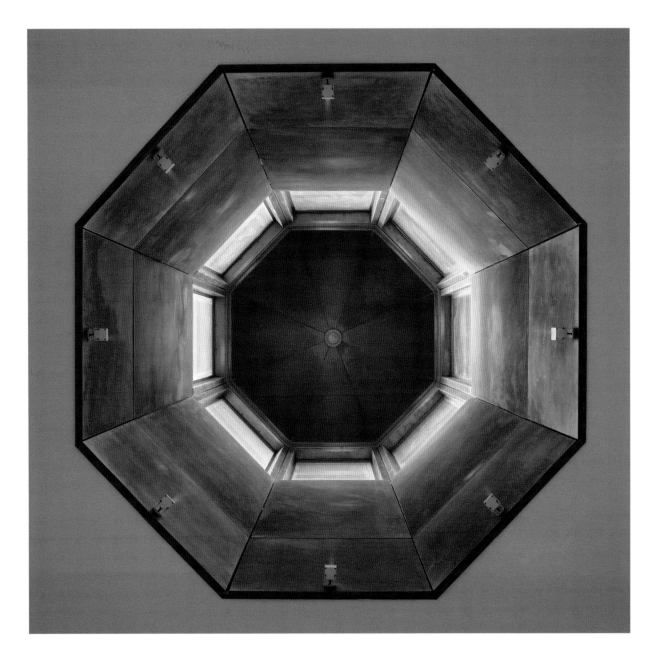

Brighton College

Opposite
Brighton College
*Our design follows
the 1885 design by TG
Jackson, but his elaborate
Jacobethan (Anglo-
Jackson they call it in
Oxford) lantern has been
replaced by a simpler,
geometrically pure, design.*

Top
*View looking up into the
new lantern.*

Our work at Brighton College makes a rather different response to context. TG Jackson designed the entrance gateway in the 1880's in brick and terracotta as a Tudor style gatehouse, but the tower was never completed owing to financial constraints. The gatehouse was thereby truncated at roof-top height in a very unfortunate manner. In recent years, the College has had one of the most ambitious buildings programmes of any school, with new buildings by Allies and Morrison, Eric Parry, Hopkins and OMA, and it was now intended to complete the unfinished tower to crown the entrance, providing a study for the headmaster overlooking the college to the north and the sea to the south, where he could meet parents and students. The relationship of our new work to the original, unexecuted design,

posed a conundrum, not least since TG Jackson had designed an extremely elaborate Jacobethan lantern, presumably of lead-clad timber, that would not have long survived the aggressive marine climate. We therefore chose to complete the integrity of the masonry shell with brick and terracotta broadly as intended by TG Jackson with sold walls and internal cork insulation. We redesigned the cupola stripped down to its octagonal geometric essence as a steel structure that could be prefabricated and dropped in by crane, then clad with copper and surmounted by a weather vane of a pelican, the school's emblem. It is remarkable how our new tower immediately became the main identifying symbol of the school, the background to their publicity shots and celebrations.

Top left
Brighton College
The tower in its incomplete state.

Top right
TG Jackson's florid unexecuted design of the 1880's.

Bottom left
Interior of the Headmaster's meeting room in the tower.

Bottom right
Celebrating the exam results: the tower has become the defining image of the school.

Opposite
Brighton College's newly completed tower seen from the school. Its new lead-clad steel-framed cupola was lifted in by crane.

Double page over
The tower dominates the entrance quad.

Toynbee Hall

The context for our work at Toynbee Hall could not be more different – a landlocked site in Whitechapel, and an urban oasis built in the 1880's in the midst of the 'vicious' East End, as defined in Charles Booth's poverty map of 1898. Toynbee Hall was founded as a University Settlement, where graduates of Oxford and Cambridge might volunteer as residents to give education and training to the local poor under the direction of Canon Barnett and his wife Henrietta Barnett. The building of 1885 was designed by Ebenezer Hoole in the style of a Tudor manor house, with a lecture hall and communal dining and sitting rooms on the ground floor, and bedrooms on the upper floors. Surprisingly, early prints show furnishings in the latest fashionable Aesthetic Movement taste, with black ebonised furniture and a remarkable proto-Art Nouveau balustrade to the staircase with fretted foliage.

Over the years Toynbee Hall has hosted many key conferences about social welfare and it still carries out a wide social role, but the facilities provided by the building needed reinvention for present day uses with superior conference and education provision on the ground floor, offices on the first floor, and a flat for short-term visitors in the attic. Our key intervention was to amalgamate three rooms to create a new main entrance and a large entrance hall visible from the street. This leads to a new circulation spine running alongside the back wall of the original building, its scarred brickwork left visible as a memory and as a means of orientation. The circulation spine mediates between the old building with its two large and one small gable, and our new extension which has a double rhythm of five small gables. We intended this as a homage to the Arts and Crafts movement, notably the gables of Philip Webb's Standen. We were inspired to do so by the example of CR Ashbee who was a volunteer at Toynbee Hall when he decorated Ashbee Hall and founded the Guild and School of Handicraft.

Top
Toynbee Hall
Ebenezer Hoole's 1885 design for Toynbee Hall, showing the three gables facing the forecourt, originally set back behind a gatehouse on Commercial Street.

Middle
Our design for the rear elevation has five gables in double-rhythm with the original gables behind.

Bottom
Toynbee Hall was notable for the volunteers from Oxford and Cambridge, who lived in Aesthetic interiors away from the squalor of Whitechapel, surrounded by Japanese screens and black ebonised Godwinesque chairs.

Top
Front courtyard with the new main entrance formed by lowering the window of one of the former bedrooms.

Middle left
The staircase is remarkable for its Mackmurdo-like fretted balustrade.

Middle right
Ashbee Hall is named after CR Ashbee, who with other volunteers redecorated the hall with roundels portraying the Tree of Life.

Bottom left
The main circulation corridor runs outside the rear red brick wall of the original building, providing easy orientation for visitors and a view of the full height of the rear elevation through a glazed margin to the floor and roof.

Bottom right
The corridor at first floor level.

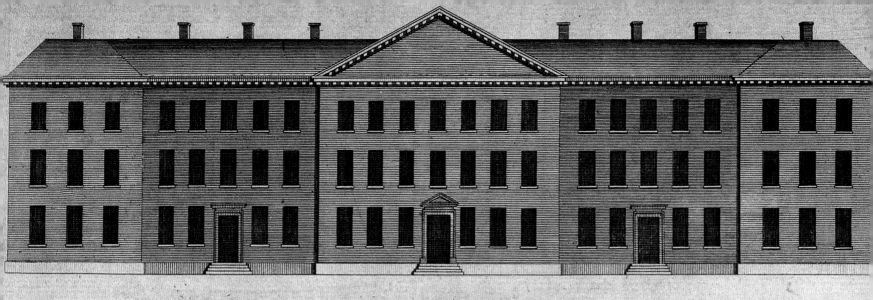

The London Hospital in Whitechapel Road.

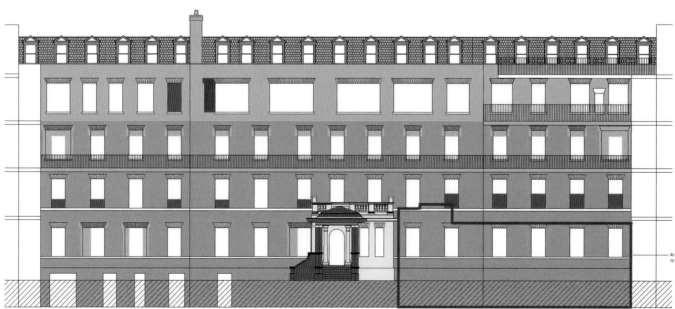

86

Opposite, top
The Royal London Hospital
The appearance of the London Hospital in 1753, three stories with a central pediment.

Opposite, middle
The rear elevation in 2017 with the addition of extra attic floors, balconies and pipework.

Opposite, bottom
An analysis of the existing fabric of the rear elevation by date reveals the extraordinary and unsuspected degree of survival of the original Georgian rear elevation. This is repaired to reflect the Georgian and later layers of history, and to retain a memory of the scars of time and the texture of age.

Key
Blue   1750's fabric
Yellow   1860's fabric
Orange 1900's fabric
Red   1970's fabric

Top
The decayed timber panels in the abandoned chapel form a triptych of great beauty.

Right
A full height atrium links the former hospital and the new Town Hall buildings.

The Royal London Hospital

While at Toynbee Hall Ashbee became involved in seeking out historic buildings in east London, leading to the saving of the Trinity Almshouses on Mile End Road, Eastbury Manor and other buildings threatened with demolition, and to the establishment of the Survey of London. East London proved a rich hunting ground for him, as it has for me when working with Julian Harrap and subsequently in my own practice. One of the most surprising discoveries for me was the Old Royal London Hospital on Whitechapel High Street when I joined the architects AHMM and their team for the design of its conversion to the new Tower Hamlets Town Hall. I had no idea that the 23 bay Georgian Hospital building of the 1750's still substantially survived, hidden behind the 19th century wings, the 1890's chapel extension, the rooftop operating theatres, the enlarged window openings, the new fenestration, the added rear balconies, and the festoons of pipes and ducts. The central part of the front elevation was obscured by the building of the chapel wing, but the rear elevation survived remarkably intact, as is apparent from the coloured-up phasing drawing.

The Borough had commissioned a feasibility study that advocated the demolition of the rear half of the Georgian hospital building, consisting of rooms either side of a longitudinal corridor, smaller rooms to the north and larger wards to the south. This would have required the demolition of most of the historic building, as well as the loss of the relatively intact rear elevation. We therefore helped to devise an alternative approach, keeping and repairing the whole of the surviving Georgian hospital building as meeting and conference rooms, separated from a Z-shaped new building by a full height glazed atrium revealing the repaired original rear elevation. The new building contains publicly

accessible uses on the whole of the ground floor, including the Council Chamber. The open plan offices above overlook the repaired and revealed elevation of the Georgian hospital.

More controversial was the decision to build a new building behind the retained façade of the Victorian Grocers' wing, with its roof rebuilt in facsimile abutting the taller new building behind. This decision was taken largely because of the need to make a public entrance to the library and town hall services through the front elevation. Instead of forming a large hole through the historic façade, the external ground is lowered instead, and a new wide glazed entrance made below. This gives access to the whole of the ground floor via steps and gentle ramps.

CHAPTER NINE

The typology of barns

I am fascinated by the typology of barns. The single cell rectangular space is the elemental building block of architecture, going back to the origins of shelter. The Abbé Laugier's account of the Primitive Hut enlivened theoretical debate in the 18th century about how to rejuvenate architecture from first principles. The Primitive Hut consisted of trees, or posts, supporting a pitched roof with triangular gables at each end: this is also the form of the vernacular barn and, in more elaborated form, that of the Greek temple. The basic form can be extended by the addition of an aisle or a lean-to, under the same roof or a roof extended at lower pitch (a catslide roof), or by the addition of a bay. Internally, the essence of the barn typology is a single volume space, or a set of linked spaces. The Arts and Crafts architects were masters of the barn typology, and some of their most notable creations are barn-like in appearance – Lethaby's Brockhampton church, ES Prior's St Andrew's Roker, and Ernest Gimson's masterpiece, the library at Bedales School. Then there are the Arts and Crafts houses, a long range of south-facing rooms entered from a corridor to the north, with, in the case of the extraordinary houses by Baillie Scott, a linkage between the rooms with timber-lined openings that provides free-flowing space throughout the ground floor. These are the interiors that helped inspire Frank Lloyd Wright in the creation of the Prairie houses; indeed, Frank Lloyd Wright and CR Ashbee were close friends.

Opposite
Kenilworth Castle
Our new ticket building acts as a threshold to the historic castle site.

Right
The Abbé Laugier's Primitive Hut from his Essai sur l'Architecture of 1753, a hugely influential work for renewing Architecture by tracing it back to its origins.

Top right
Ernest Gimson's Arts and Crafts library at Bedales School of 1911 has massive oak timbers and gloriously wide floorboards cut as slices of an oak tree.

Bottom right
Frank Lloyd Wright's Zimmerman House of 1951 has long horizontals at sill, head and eaves level.

Kenilworth Castle

We were appointed by English Heritage at Kenilworth Castle to design a new ticket office and shop at the entrance to the site from the car park, on the site of the ruined Gallery Tower. English Heritage had already obtained designs for a contemporary pavilion when they decided to re-write the brief to require a timber-framed building *such as would have been characteristic of castle sites in medieval times.* We were happy to oblige with a primitive hut, or barn, built with green oak compression members, steel bar tension members (in order to keep as spacious an internal appearance as possible), oak plank walls, and an oak shingle roof. A raised central lantern gives light to the interior, and its gables extend down the full height of the end walls as oak-louvred windows. The building flanks the visitor entrance to the site across a bridge over the Great Mere that surrounded the castle and made it impregnable. Our new building recreates a sense of enclosure between it and the ruined walls of the Gallery Tower, as one of several successive thresholds of entrance to the castle.

Kenilworth Castle is in fact owned by Kenilworth Council and is only managed by English Heritage. A vocal objector at the public meeting furiously attacked our building as a blot on the landscape, and the local paper vilified it as a 'chicken shed'. I felt sympathy for Inigo Jones when the Duke of Bedford asked for a barn-like building at St Paul's Covent Garden: he said that in that case he would give him 'the finest barn in Christendom'. I am pleased that ours may be the finest chicken shed in Christendom. Once complete, it was welcomed by local residents and won a Warwickshire Design Award.

Top
Kenilworth Castle
The Kenilworth Castle ticket office and shop has an oak frame, oak planks and an oak shingle roof.

Bottom
The interior of the ticket office and shop.

Lincoln's Inn Fields

In 2007 we were commissioned to produce a sketch design for a new café in Lincoln's Inn Fields by Camden Council, and proposed a long, low pavilion against the main path to the north, overlooking the tennis courts to the south. The pavilion took the form of a gabled barn with laminated timber cruck frames and fully opening glazed oak doors on the long sides. The pavilion was designed with a low-pitched copper roof and with a raised floor so that the pavilion appeared to float above the ground. We were asked to present a model to the Lincoln's Inn Association, which was in favour of the design and of the proposed location, albeit different from that intended in the brief. I was therefore surprised to receive a phone call a few years later asking about the pavilion that had just been built for the Council on a design-and-build contract, without planning consent. I visited and found that our concept had been followed, without reference to us. It has hefty timber ties that block long views of the interior rather than cruck frames that would have kept the view unobstructed, and it lacks the bays at each end that would have avoided monotony. The council could have done much better for the public.

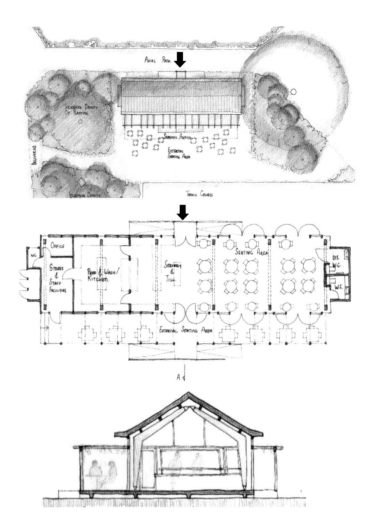

Top
Site plan with terrace overlooking the tennis courts.

Upper middle
Plan and section of the new cafe.

Lower middle
View of the entrance from the E-W path.

Bottom
View of the cafe that was let as a design-and-build contract by the Council.

Whitehouse Barns, Suffolk

I have had great enjoyment in exploring the barn typology at Whitehouse Barns, near Blythburgh in Suffolk, since my purchase in 2001 of two acres of land overlooking the floodplain of the river Blyth between Southwold and Walberswick. The land was formerly the dairy farm of the Henham Estate, and was covered with the rubble of demolished buildings, and the derelict remains of four barns. The central barn, built of concrete block, consisted of two storage rooms and an open-fronted vehicle shed, 93 feet long and 15 feet wide. I set myself the task of creating two holiday barns, Upper Barn from the two storage rooms, and Lower Barn from the vehicle shed, linked by a single utility room and two doors, so that the barns could be let separately or together, and so that the ceiling of each barn could be seen to its full length. In the case of Upper Barn, this was achieved by having a gallery bedroom overlooking the sitting room, and in Lower Barn it was achieved by having curtained sleeping balconies at both ends. In each barn further bedrooms are situated below the galleries. A catslide roof on the entrance side provides smaller spaces – halls, toilets, bathrooms and utility room – that allow the main area to be as large and unobstructed as possible. A conceit is the shutters: these are lined with red-stained planks when open, and with black-stained boards when shut, so that the whole building reverts to a black clapboarded barn.

Top
Whitehouse Barns
after conversion for holiday use. The shutters form an abstract composition of red rectangles.

Middle
The barns before work started.

Bottom
The floodplain of the river Blyth at low-tide.

92

Drift Barn, Suffolk

More recently we obtained consent to convert the timber-frame clapboarded Drift Barn in the north-west corner of the site, enjoying the best views of the estuary, into a holiday barn for ourselves. The concept here is the insertion within the shell of the existing barn of a new highly insulated timber-frame building with high specification sliding glazed doors lining up with the barn doors, which open as shutters. The boards have been retained in their rustic state, acting as a rainscreen cladding. The rusty corrugated iron roof has been replaced with a new rusty corrugated Corten steel roof, with an inset rectangle of black photovoltaic panels, inspired by Rothko. Inside, the rectangle of the barn is divided into four: a bedroom and shower room at each end, and a two-bay living/dining/kitchen in the middle, made of walnut joinery and black Corian worktops. To the north, there are three Baillie Scott-like recesses for the entrance, the piano and the utilities. A horizontal walnut batten runs continuously at door head level, inspired by Frank Lloyd Wright. This separates the panels of walnut and clay plaster below from the white frieze and ceiling above, recreating a medieval wall articulation in a contemporary manner.

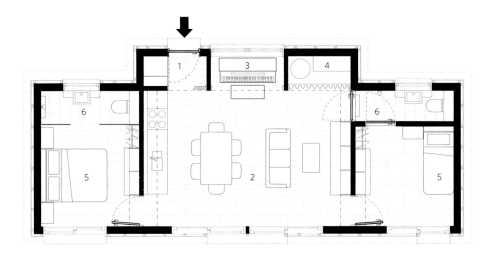

Top
Drift Barn a*fter conversion, with new Corten roof and photovaltaic panels.*

Middle
Plan of Drift Barn showing the entrance, piano and utility recesses, with slate-lined shower rooms opening off each bedroom.

Key
1   Hall
2   Kitchen/Living
3   Piano
4   Utility
5   Bedroom
6   Shower room

Above
Drift Barn before work started with its rusty corrugated iron roof.

Top
The interior of Drift Barn has a walnut floor and doors, French clay plaster walls, and a plain white frieze and ceiling.

Left
The internal face of the external boarding can be seen through the glazed doors of the barn.

Far left
The slate-lined shower room.

Opposite
Fitted walnut display shelves with sleeping balcony above.

CHAPTER TEN

The art of repair and the texture of age

That which I have insisted upon as the life of the whole, that spirit which is given only by the hand and eye of the workman, can never be recalled...and as for direct and simple copying , it is palpably impossible. What copying can there be of surfaces that have been worn half an inch down? The whole finish was in that half inch that is gone; if you attempt to restore that finish you do so conjecturally; if you copy what is left, how is the new work better than the old?
Ruskin, *The Seven Lamps of Architecture*, 1849

The ruin is magnificent, unimaginable; it is a ruin the colour of sapphire, rubies, emerald; a ruin that blinds one by the beauty of the agatization of the stone fired by kerosene. With its empty niches, its shattered or damaged statues, its remains of a clock, its high window frames and chimneys, standing upright by some miracle of balance in empty space against the blue sky, this ruin would be a marvel of the picturesque to preserve, if the country were not condemned, without appeal, to the restorations of M. Viollet-le-Duc.
The Journal of the de Goncourts, 1871, on the burnt-out Hôtel de Ville in Paris

I have always taken the view that the repair of historic buildings is an aesthetic as well as a technical matter. In particular, the texture of age has a fundamental significance for old buildings, that grows with time, and that is absent from new buildings. For Ruskin, the weathered surface of a building bore witness to historical memory and to the hand of the workman; for the de Goncourts it was a purely aesthetic reaction; but, either way, decisions about repair are necessarily architectural decisions that must pay due regard to both points of view.

Stonework

The approach to repair in this country has been largely shaped by the Society for the Protection of Ancient Buildings (SPAB), founded by William Morris in 1877, and developed by Philip Webb, AR Powys, William Weir and others. In the early years the SPAB architects made a moralistic principle of not replacing a material with the same material for fear of deception, for example by using tile and mortar repairs to decayed stonework. However, this approach was abandoned following the realisation that the weathering pattern of tiles was fundamentally different from that of stonework, and the new convention became like-for-like replacement. Nevertheless, we have used tile and mortar repair ourselves, using stone rather than clay tiles, in the consolidation of ruined masonry at Gloucester Blackfriars.

Opposite
Garrick Club
Detail of the three types of render – the original render; our new render coat with ashlaring; and the original precast elements to the cornice.

Right
Gloucester Blackfriars
Stone tiles were used to consolidate the ruined masonry.

We consider that the repair of masonry walls is an aesthetic and technical matter that calls for a range of approaches according to circumstance, and to the architecture and history of the building.

At one extreme are the great medieval cathedrals with surviving original stonework. When I was appointed Cathedral Architect at **St Albans Abbey** in 2000, I changed the stone repair policy to one of maximum retention and minimum intervention of the medieval soft clunch stonework. This involved cleaning superficial dirt, re-pointing open joints with lime mortar, applying a lime shelter-coat and fitting lead caps dressed to throw rainwater clear of the tas-de-charge, the springing points of the lost vaults of the monastic cloister. Startlingly bright at first, the limewash rapidly weathered to achieve an aesthetic balance with the walls of brick and flint, giving a warm glow when seen from the Abbey Orchard. By contrast we replaced the damaged or missing stone seats within the bays of the cloister, facing a new public walkway against the south front of the Abbey and looking out over Abbey Orchard to the site of the Roman Verulamium at the bottom of the hill.

The decay of sandstone, which was by George Gwilt in his refacing of the eastern used parts of **Southwark Cathedral** in the 1840's, is fundamentally different to the decay of limestone, and is characterised by rounded edges of decay to all the blocks. These had been pointed in the 20th century with ugly cement mortar fillets up to 50mm wide. We were able to remove the cement pointing and to reveal the original joints of extraordinary fineness – as little as 2mm – without any need for re-pointing.

Stonework *that has been worn half an inch down* may be conserved, but, where the loss is much greater, replacement may be necessary. This is particularly true of classical buildings with walls of coursed ashlar, such as Hawksmoor's **St Alfege, Greenwich**, where we replaced whole blocks, whose corners had been fractured by the expansion of embedded iron cramps, in order to retain the stern architectural quality of Hawksmoor's architecture.

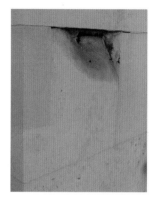
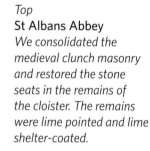

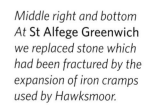

Top
St Albans Abbey
We consolidated the medieval clunch masonry and restored the stone seats in the remains of the cloister. The remains were lime pointed and lime shelter-coated.

Middle left
Southwark Cathedral
The stone refacing carried out by George Gwilt on the eastern parts of the then parish Church of St Saviour, used sandstone with 2mm joints, later obscured by crude 20th century pointing. We removed the hard cement re-pointing seen here to reveal the original fine joint width.

Middle right and bottom
At **St Alfege Greenwich** *we replaced stone which had been fractured by the expansion of iron cramps used by Hawksmoor.*

Brickwork

As with stone buildings, brick buildings have been extensively damaged in the past by being re-pointed with hard cement mortar. This has the effect of trapping rainwater, which then has to dry out through the brick rather than through a softer lime mortar joint, with the consequent risk of frost damage in winter. This was dramatically the case on the west elevation of **Eastbury Manor,** where the whole face of the brick to a depth of an inch had fractured and had to be removed. Rather than refacing the whole area, we re-pointed with soft lime mortar the fractured brickwork, following the eroded profile of the brick. The eroded brick so exposed is still three inches thick and therefore structurally sound. Fifteen years later it is still in good condition.

Cleaning

A fundamental consideration in the repair of masonry buildings is that of cleaning, an issue with major technical and aesthetic ramifications. The thick encrustations of soot that once gave the 18th century Portland stone churches by Hawksmoor and others such character are now an endangered species. At the **Garrick Club** we faced a dilemma, since the cleaning of the rendered front elevation had been halted by English Heritage a few years prior to our appointment, on the grounds that the soot-encrusted elevation of what had come to be known as *the dirtiest building in London* was of significance in its own right. A condition survey revealed serious cracking of the render of the upper façade, and demonstrated that cleaning had to be carried out for technical as well as aesthetic reasons before the cracks could be cut out and filled with lime render. We also applied an additional thin coat of lime render to the flat parts of the upper elevation, and lined it out to resemble ashlar masonry as intended by the architect, Marable, and as shown in the watercolour view of his design. This extra coat of render is of a lighter colour than the render of the remainder of the elevation, which consists of a mixture of in situ and precast elements, and enhances the appearance of Marable's Italian Renaissance Palazzo.

Top
Eastbury Manor
We removed the whole brick face that had fractured to a depth of 25mm and re-pointed with a soft lime mortar following the eroded profile.

Middle
Garrick Club
Marable's watercolour view of 1862 showing the intended ashlaring.

Bottom
The soot-encrusted facade before cleaning and repair. The Garrick Club was known as 'the dirtiest building in London'.

Double page over Cleaning and repair brought out the contrasting colours of the original render to the plinth and window surrounds, the new render to the piano nobile and balustrade, and the original pre-cast brackets and ornament.

Cleaning can also be vital to restoring an architect's original intentions. In the late 19th century Norman Shaw devised an attractive style based on the use of red brick with bands of Portland stone masonry and green Westmoreland slate roofs, as can be seen for example at New Scotland Yard, yet the colour contrast is entirely lost on a sooty facade. In conjunction with Eric Parry's interior remodelling of the Hyde Park Hotel, we cleaned the red brick and stone dressings of the front elevation. We also restored the roof slopes by replacing their grey Welsh slates with green Westmoreland slates, as featured in the original design. Red and green are complementary colours, and the combination of red and green in architecture has a long ancestry deriving from the neo-classical discovery of Pompeii and Herculaneum, with their red frescoes and patinated bronze doors.

Wrought Iron

The repair of ironwork has its own set of technical and aesthetic problems. Wrought iron rusts and expands in reaction with water to a volume seven times greater than the original, with inexorable force. It was impressive to witness at Hawksmoor's St Alfege, Greenwich how the whole of the large Roman altars at the east end of the church had been jacked up by two inches or more by the built-in ends of the wrought iron railings. As with masonry, having removed the laminations of rust, eroded wrought iron has its own inimitable character. With railings, repair or replacement may be unavoidable for safety reasons. However, at St George's Tower, Oxford Castle, a Scheduled Ancient Monument of Saxon date adjacent to the Norman castle mound, we could take an extreme preservationist approach to repair since the tower is only used by visitors climbing to obtain the panoramic view of the towers and spires of Oxford from our viewing gallery on the roof. The wrought iron bars, or ferramenta, of the windows in the massively thick walls of the tower were eroded to nothing where they had been built into the sills, yet we still managed to retain them without repair by holding them by means of new horizontal bars fitted within the window embrasure.

Top left
The front elevation of the Hyde Park Hotel following cleaning of the Portland stone and red brick and re-roofing with green Westmoreland slate.

Bottom left
The railings and stone altars at St Alfege Greenwich, before and after replacement of the embedded iron, conservation and lime shelter-coating.

Opposite top row
The cast iron dovetail cramps at the Granary Building King's Cross had caused splitting of the whole of the massive granite coping stones.

Opposite middle rows
The defective eaves detail at St Luke's Oseney Crescent, the damage it caused, and the church after replacement of wall plates, rafter ends, new cast iron gutters and downpipes.

Opposite bottom row
New doorway in the conserved medieval fabric of Gloucester Blackfriars, and floorboards retained behind the rebuilt elevation.

Cast Iron

By contrast to wrought iron, cast iron is generally assumed to be inert, yet this proved not to be the case at the **Granary building, King's Cross.** We struggled to understand why the massive granite stones of the parapet had all split diagonally at the corners, until we discovered that the stones had been joined by means of dovetail cast iron cramps set into close-cut sockets in the tops of the stones, whose expansion, though small, had been sufficient to split the massive granite blocks.

Structure

St Luke's, Oseney Crescent in Kentish Town was the first work of Basil Champneys, best known for his Queen Anne style buildings at Newnham College, Cambridge. His design failures at St Luke's are a result of his inexperience. The nave arcade was inadequately buttressed at the west end against the thrust of the arches, with consequent large cracks in the final, western, bay of the arcade. We tied the whole arcade by drilling the arches at springing level and inserting stainless steel bars from one end to the other, jointed within the piers, and tied to the cross walls at each end.

Redesign

Champneys had laid gutters directly onto the wall head, with horizontal lead gutters leading to downpipes at each end. These had allowed water to penetrate, damaging the wall heads, and leading to serious decay of the ends of the timber trusses. The only way to effect a long-term cure was to redesign the roof with a shallower pitch at the eaves, leading to new external cast iron gutters and downpipes at each bay of the nave.

Rebuilding

The terrace of Regency houses built into the remains of the **Gloucester Blackfriars** had been decaying for 20 years and the front elevation was on the point of collapse when we were appointed to restore them. This involved the rebuilding of the upper part of the elevation, the conservation of the medieval doorway and the insertion of a new glazed door. Inside the houses we managed to retain and piece in the floorboarding despite the rebuilding of the elevation.

CHAPTER ELEVEN

The art of construction and detailing

Dealing as it did with the common facts of building in scores and hundreds of examples, it (the Society for the Protection of Ancient Buildings) became under the technical guidance of Philip Webb, the architect, a real school of practical building – architecture with all the whims which we usually call 'design' left out. It is a curious fact that this Society, engaged in an intense study of antiquity, became a school of rational builders and modern building.
William Lethaby, *Ernest Gimson: His Life and Work*, 1924

In all its work, Richard Griffiths Architects remain true to the creation of a timeless architecture, in which style derives from materials, use and construction rather than from the whims of fashion.
Richard Griffiths Architects' manifesto

Lethaby draws attention to how the architecture of the Arts and Crafts was based on an intense study of old buildings, the materials from which they were made, their means of construction, and the way in which they weathered over time. The emphasis on building using local materials and sustainable construction still has much to teach us today, as we look for more ecologically sound and enduring methods of construction, for buildings better integrated into their local environment, and for buildings that gather texture and richness as they grow older. The study of old buildings can suggest a middle way between the twin extremes of minimalism – Mies van der Rohe's 'less is more' – and maximalism – Robert Venturi's 'less is a bore'.

Our manifesto refers to an architecture founded on construction and materials, and our preferred means of expression for our new design work is exposed construction and self-finished materials. In this, we follow the Arts and Crafts architects in finding inspiration in medieval and vernacular buildings, with their more primitive forms, local materials and expressed construction; but we are also inspired by the primitive architecture of the great 19th century warehouse and industrial buildings on which we have worked at the **London Dock Warehouse**, the **Ragged School Museum** and the **King's Cross Granary Building**.

Timber

We have always believed in the value of solid materials rather than composites, and like to use English stones and bricks for the innate beauty of their material, as well as native English timbers – ash, oak and walnut – for their grain and appearance, providing pattern and texture without applied decoration. The use of green oak posts, beams, boarding and roof shingles was loved by the architects of the Arts and Crafts, not least by Gimson with his magnificent oak library and Lupton Hall at **Bedales School** that we restored in 2017. Our use of green oak posts and beams and planed oak boards, usually fixed flush with shadow gaps and exposed screw fixings, gives character and attractive weathering to our new ticket office at **Kenilworth Castle** and to the arbours and aviary of the recreated Tudor Garden, as well as to our new staircase enclosure at **Eastbury Manor** and to our rebuilt Studies for **Bedales School.**

Opposite
Kenilworth Castle
The ticket office and shop at Kenilworth Castle has a frame of green oak, walls of oak boarding and a roof of oak shingles.

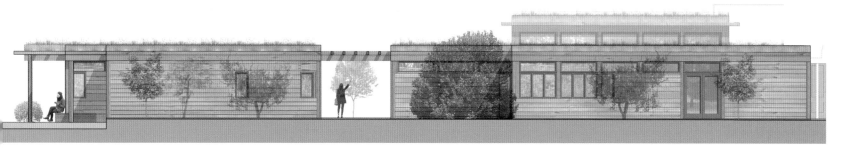

Top
The Studies at **Bedales School***, rebuilt with a modular timber frame and oak boarding similar that at Eastbury Manor and Kenilworth Castle.*

Middle left
Kenilworth Castle
Construction of the Tudor arbours.

Middle right
The staircase enclosure at **Eastbury Manor** *has an oak frame and oak flush boarding with shadow gap detailing.*

Bottom left
Ernest Gimson's library at **Bedales School** *has the most extraordinary floorboards, tapering slices of an oak tree, an inch and a half thick, forty feet long and up to thirty inches wide.*

Bottom right
The copper roofing at **Southwark Cathedral** *is beginning to patinate to a green verdigris colour, contrasting with the stone and flint of the walls and the oak and bronze-coloured steel windows.*

Top
The Corten steel roof at
Drift Barn, Suffolk *rusted
during the first rainfall and
has developed a handsome
patina.*

Bottom left
*My new stair balustrade
in the Edwardian wing of*
Sutton House.

Bottom right
*The bronze-finished
roof trusses at* **Lambeth
Palace** *have paired steel
angles grasping the tie rod
and the strut that turn the
angles into a lightweight
truss.*

Roofing

For roofing we prefer to avoid industrial roofing systems in favour of tile, slate, lead, copper or dark zinc, laid with timber rolls (lead) or standing seams (copper and zinc). At **Southwark Cathedral** our copper roofing is gradually weathering to a lovely green patination matching that on the east end of the Cathedral. At **Drift Barn** in Suffolk, in memory of the rusty corrugated iron roof that had to be replaced, we managed to source corrugated Corten steel roofing sheets that have now rusted to the same beautiful deep red rust colour.

Metalwork

For exposed metalwork we like to use bronze-finished architectural brass if the budget allows, or else steel with a bronze metallic finish. This gives an entirely different, dignified and dramatic aesthetic to the metalwork as compared with the white-painted steelwork associated with exposed high-tech construction. Bronze-finished metalwork graces the metal balustrades and ironmongery at **Sutton House,** our roof trusses at **Lambeth Palace,** and our screens and balustrades at the **London Dock Warehouse.**

Flitch detailing

For structures, we have a preference for the flitch joint, where a single member is grasped between two other members. Our most significant articulation of this language of construction was at **Southwark Cathedral.** Here, the precast concrete beams and vaults of the ground floor refectory, and the precast concrete ribs of the first floor library, are paired and joined with steel plates. The supports for the staircase balustrade consist of paired steel balusters joined by steel plates to which the cantilevered balustrade panels are connected.

The same detail is found at **Sutton House** and at **Lambeth Palace,** where the bronze-finished balustrade panels are of extreme lightness but great strength, despite the use of horizontal bars only one inch wide by a quarter inch thick. The bars are spaced four inches apart and connected vertically by means of 6mm diameter bars so that they act together structurally.

The same flitch detail is also used in relation to the steel windows and doors of the ground floor rooms and refectory at **Southwark Cathedral.** Paired steel flats form architraves to the projecting oak doors, with shadow gaps concealing thermal insulation between them. The paired steels with shadow gap continue over the head of the door, only here the upper steel flat projects as a cornice to the triple membered entablature. This provides a subliminal classical reference within the more medieval and Arts and Crafts inspiration of the building as a whole.

Door

Within the exposed construction of our buildings, and in the context of a building industry increasingly geared up to the on-site assembly of factory-made components, our scope as architects for new buildings is increasingly restricted to the choice of manufactured components and how they are assembled.

However, the one freedom that we have indulged is in the design of doors, and the five-plank door has acquired a special status in the office. Inspired originally by the surviving Tudor door to the Summer Parlour at **Eastbury Manor,** it consists of five vertical planks on one side of the

Top row
The roof trusses in the library at **Southwark Cathedral** *consist of paired pre-cast concrete crucks, linked by a steel flitch plate.*

Second row left
The staircase balustrades at **Southwark Cathedral** *also have paired steel balusters supporting cantilevered glass balustrade panels.*

Second row right
The balustrade to the bridge at **Lambeth Palace** *that spans the courtyard has cantilevered balustrade panels with the thinnest possible bronze horizontal bars linked structurally by means of 6mm diameter rods.*

Third row
The door frame architraves at **Southwark Cathedral** *have paired steel plates separated by a 6mm shadow gap hiding the insulation. At the top of the door the chamfered top plate projects as a cornice to the virtual entablature.*

Bottom row
Hinged lengths of floor board give access to electrical sockets at **Eastbury Manor.**

The surviving Tudor door at **Eastbury Manor** *to the Summer Parlour with vertical planks to the front face and horizontal planks to the rear face, clenched together.*

Rear view of the Tudor door at **Eastbury Manor.**

The basic five plank door at **Sutton House** *set in a bronze frame.*

Variant with vertical square gridded vision panel at **Queen Elizabeth's Walk.**

Fully glazed doors at **Burghley Brewhouse.**

Door with vertical planks to the front face and horizontal planks to the rear face framing a square vision panel at **Drift Barn.**

door and either five vertical or ten horizontal planks on the other. The square where the planks overlap can form a small vision panel, or the vision panel can replace one, two or three whole vertical planks on the front of the door. This versatile door typology graces nearly all our new buildings, as various as **Sutton House, Southwark Cathedral, Lambeth Palace** and **Drift Barn.**

Services

Perhaps the most challenging aspect of design in the reuse of old buildings is in the integration of new services, owing to the ever-increasing scope and complexity of the servicing requirements. Great efforts may be made to exploit every void in the historic building to accommodate services with the minimum visual impact, even though this may mean a greater physical and archaeological impact in accessing those voids. Such was the case at Sutton House and at Eastbury where the power sockets were hidden below hinged pieces of floor board. Alternatively, the services may be exposed, in which case their visual impact is itself a matter of sensitive design. At the Ragged School Museum circular conduits were used rather than trunking in view of their smaller visual impact despite their greater number. I also find that exposed services can be made acceptable, if they are run in the corners of the space rather than centrally.

Above
Exposed electrical trunking at the **Ragged School Museum.**

CHAPTER TWELVE

Architecture and decoration

One of the revelations of working with historic buildings is that decoration is integral to architectural style and not merely a matter of personal taste. In other words, decoration is a means to an architectural end, and not an end in itself. This was reinforced in earlier centuries because the cost of different pigments varied enormously, and some were of exotic origin – ultramarine from lapis lazuli in Afghanistan, carmine from cochineal beetles in America – and therefore reflected status and wealth. I have always considered decoration to be an essential and fascinating part of architecture.

Jesus College, Cambridge

My first opportunity to grapple with the issue was in the redecoration of the College Hall at Jesus College, Cambridge. The hall is a medieval survival of the pre-Dissolution Nunnery of St Radegund, and was fitted with classical panelling by Grumbold in the early 18th century. The panelling of the hall had been stripped and redecorated by David Roberts in the 1970's in a dark brown colour, and I was appointed to design a redecoration scheme, a relighting scheme, and a high table servery, in time for the College's quincentenary in 1996. It was clear that the existing scheme was not liked, and that a new scheme should relate to the classical language of the panelling. This could of course have been done in a plain colour, as in the redecoration of the hall at Magdalene, but the richness of articulation of the panelling at Jesus College suggested a richer decorative scheme, such as those by Hugh May at Windsor Castle of the 1680's, which were recorded in *Pyne's Royal Residences* of 1819 before their destruction.

Opposite
Russian Orthodox Cathedral
The columns of the nave are decorated in imitation of porphyry, the purple igneous stone found in Egypt and much prized by the Roman Emperors.

Right
Jesus College, Cambridge
Our watercolour designs for the redecoration of the entrance screen and the high table panelling.

Grumbold's panelling extends around all four sides of the hall, but at the entrance screen and at the high table end a Corinthian colonnade is superimposed in front of the panelling, and there are panelled doors with wide architraves. I chose a decorative scheme to reflect this hierarchy, with two stone colours for the panelling, a marbled colonnade with a richer marble for the frieze, and walnut-grained doors with marble architraves matching those of the entablature. Gold leaf was used to highlight the flutes of the columns, the acanthus tips of the column capitals, and a single moulding of the panelling, making a wonderful effect during candle-lit dinners. The work had to be carried out during the eight-week Summer holiday, with a conference of all the Commonwealth Chief Justices starting on the following Monday morning. This was achieved by the builders working all day, and the specialist decorators, the wonderful Huning Decorations, working all night.

Top
Hugh May's interiors at Windsor Castle of 1675, as recorded before their destruction by Wyatville.

Bottom left
Our redecoration of the hall of Jesus College, Cambridge, was inspired by May's Windsor interiors, depicting fictive marble Corinthian Order columns in front of fictive stone panelling and fictive walnut grained doors.

Bottom right
Detail of the high table screen.

Opposite
The magnificent Benin bronze cockerel, a rebus on the name of Bishop Alcock, the 15th century founder, was given pride of place between the doors of the screen. It has subsequently been removed because of its political sensitivity. It should be replaced, with a copy if necessary.

Russian Orthodox Cathedral

At the Russian Orthodox Cathedral in Ennismore Gardens, converted in the 1920's from a Victorian Anglican Church by Vulliamy and Harrison Townsend, the problem was similar. However, in this case the whole of the white-painted interior and the wonderful sgraffito frieze added by Haywood Sumner in 1900 was covered in soot from the candles that are burnt in great numbers. Paint research revealed that Harrison Townsend had painted the columns in a rich red colour, and we proposed the use of porphyry graining, stimulated by the richness of the church interiors in St Petersburg and the imperial significance of porphyry in Roman and early Christian interiors. The porphyry colour contrasts with the stone colour of the walls and the rich reds and blues of Heywood Sumner's sgraffito work, and is set off by highlights of gilded decoration on the capitals of the columns.

The nave of the Cathedral is of three bays, and we proposed lighting by means of three large new chandeliers, one in the centre of each bay, again inspired by early Christian precedent, notably Hagia Sophia in Constantinople. The chandeliers are made of hoops of copper, perforated with

Greek crosses, held between hoops of brass. This gives a colour combination reflecting that of the apse, with its gilded quarter dome and its copper frieze band. Candle bulbs are suspended from the hoops, which are linked by bars, again in the shape of a Greek cross, supporting four downlights giving light to the lectern below.

The references to the early Christian church proved apposite in the light of our experience during the project. One day, we received a letter saying that any instructions purporting to be issued on behalf of the Russian Orthodox Cathedral were not issued with their authority and should be ignored. It transpired that this was a consequence of the schism between the old White Russians who had founded the Cathedral after the Revolution, and the new incoming Red Russians who wanted to take the Cathedral back into the Patriarchate of Moscow. The reaction of the Bishop and former members of the congregation was to try and take the Cathedral back into the even more ancient Greek Orthodox Church, under the Patriarchate of Constantinople. The Red Russians prevailed.

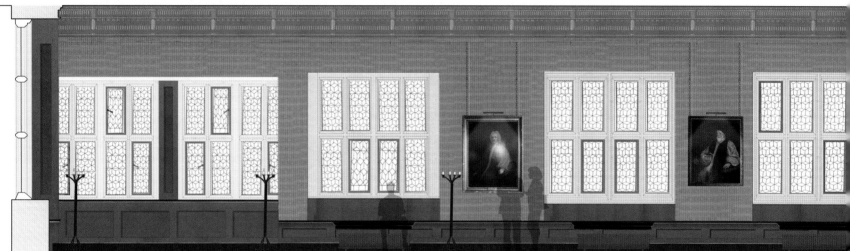

The Charterhouse

The Charterhouse is a most extraordinary survival in Clerkenwell, an almshouse for fifty Brothers who have fallen on hard times. We assisted in a period of great change and renewal, preparing a Condition Survey, a Conservation Management Plan, plans for the creation of new Brothers' rooms and offices, and an appraisal of options for new development within the grounds. We then won a competition for the 'beautification and refreshment' of the Great Chamber. This splendid room is a survival of the Tudor mansion that replaced the Carthusian Monastery following the Dissolution. It is the largest Great Chamber in the country, and the room where Elizabeth first sat in state when she became queen. The magnificent black and gold chimney piece dates from this period, flanked by pairs of columns on a grey-green plinth. The room was burnt out in the Second World War and reconstructed by Seeley and Paget with an embossed wallpaper as a background to tapestries. Following the completion of Eric Parry's Opening up the Charterhouse project it had been decided to reinvent the Great Chamber as a gallery for the display of their fine collection of 17th and 18th century portraits of Governors, and shown to visitors as part of their tour. The room was also to house a six-week summer exhibition, and at all times to act as the primary space for functions, dinners, concerts and receptions.

Our architectural vision for the redecoration of the room was shaped by the surviving Tudor chimneypiece. At first I wanted to paint the deep cornice (designed by Bore in the 1840's) and the dado panelling in black with gold highlights to match the chimneypiece columns, as in Aesthetic interiors such as Leighton House. In the event, we modified the contrast by painting the cornice and panelling grey-green as the chimneypiece plinth, with a black skirting and dado rail and gold highlights. The dado and cornice serve to frame the wall surface which is lined with a rich green linen and silk moiré fabric and provides a wonderful background to the portraits. The windows and window reveals are finished with a stone-coloured limewash, and the existing ceiling painting is simplified to plain white with coloured heraldic shields. Gold leaf is reserved for the enrichments in the north recess where Elizabeth 1 would have sat in state. In this manner we hope to unify the architecture of the room as a background to the 17th-century portraits.

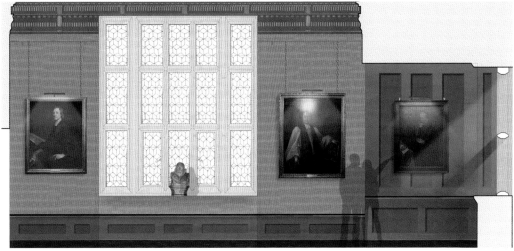

Top
The Charterhouse
Our proposal for redecoration, taking its cue from the decoration of the great Tudor chimneypiece. A green silk and linen moirée fabric has been chosen to line the walls and to provide a suitable background for the display of the 17th century portraits of governors.

Left
The Great Chamber of the Charterhouse as reconstructed after the WW2 by Seeley and Paget with wallpaper , tapestries, gilded ceiling and Festival of Britain-style light fittings.

CHAPTER THIRTEEN

New uses for old buildings

At the principal door of St. Sophia, he (Mehmet the Conqueror) alighted from his horse and entered the dome; and such was his jealous regard for that monument of his glory that, on observing a zealous Musulman in the act of breaking the marble pavement, he admonished him with his scymetar that, if the spoil and captives were granted to the soldiers, the public and private buildings had been reserved for the prince. By his command the metropolis of the Eastern church was transformed into a mosch: the rich and portable instruments of superstition had been removed; the crosses were thrown down; and the walls, which were covered with images and mosaics, were washed and purified and restored to a state of naked simplicity.
Edward Gibbon, *The History of the Decline and Fall of the Roman Empire*, Chapter 68: Extinction of the Roman Empire in the East (1453)

A change of use may be dramatic, or it may be low key, or, as at Hagia Sophia under the Ottomans, it may be both at the same time. However, any successful conversion of a historic building must first address the fundamentals of accessibility, how you find the building, enter it and move around it, both horizontally and vertically, where you place the lift and how you escape in the event of fire. The requirement to adapt historic buildings to make them accessible in accordance with the Equality Act is a challenge, and one that requires a creative response to balancing the needs of the historic building with the reasonable expectations of the Act. In this regard I like to refer to the definition of what is reasonable, as set out in a famous legal judgment of 1903, namely the opinion of *the ordinary man, the reasonable man, the man on the Clapham omnibus.*

Opposite
Freston Tower, *owned by The Landmark Trust enjoys wonderful views of the estuary of the river Orwell outside Ipswich.*

The aim of the reasonable architect is as far as possible to allow everyone to enter at the same entrance, or by a separate accessible entrance leading to the same entrance hall, leading to the horizontal and vertical circulation, inevitably involving the insertion of a lift, and thence to the rooms and spaces of the building. The reuse of these rooms and spaces can then be considered, preferably on the principle of long life, loose fit, allowing for future changes. The introduction of new uses can bring an exciting new element to the enjoyment of old buildings, with a serendipitous or symbiotic relationship between the old and the new.

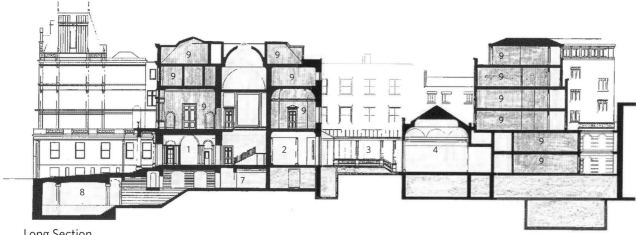

Long Section

In and Out Club

When the In and Out Club moved out of their famous premises on Piccadilly in 1999 we were asked by the new owner to obtain consent for its conversion into a 106 bed hotel, 'the finest hotel in London'. This was a fascinating exercise, involving great ingenuity in the design of a grand ground floor circulation system leading to the reused historic staircases in the five constituent buildings, with new lift cores adjacent. A Palladian villa designed by Matthew Brettingham for Lord Egremont forms the core of the building, containing the reception and the main public areas on the ground floor and the grandest suites on the upper floors. The vaulted cellars, of a Roman grandeur, were to be revealed and converted to house the spa and leisure facilities of the hotel, extending into a Byzantine cistern-like pool under the forecourt. A new building at the rear of the site was to contain further rooms served by a corridor that changes sides part way up the building, the lower rooms overlooking a courtyard to the north, the upper rooms looking south over the top of the ballroom. This project remains, as yet, unrealised.

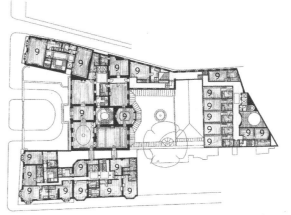

First Floor Plan

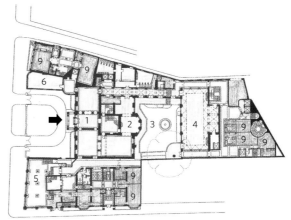

Ground Floor Plan

Top and middle rows
In and Out Club, Piccadilly
The ground floor circulation links the historic staircases and the new lift cores in the five constituent buildings. The section shows the spa in the vaulted cellars extending into a large pool below the forecourt, like a Byzantine cistern.

Key
1 Entrance
2 Lounges
3 Courtyard
4 Ballroom
5 Restaurant
6 Bar
7 Spa
8 Pool
9 Suite

Bottom
The In and Out Club, originally built as Lord Egremont's Palladian townhouse to designs by Matthew Brettingham of the 1750's.

Opposite top
Temple Church Bristol
was fire bombed in WWII and remains unroofed. Excavation has revealed the plan of the circular Templars' Church below the 15th century church of the Hospitallers.

Opposite bottom
Plan and sections of our project for rebuilding Temple Church as a glass centre for Bristol. Our proposal would have re-roofed the church with a lamella roof and inserted a bottle kiln at the centre of the circular Templars' church.

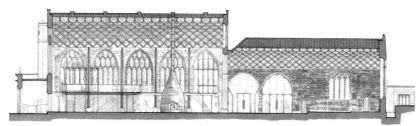

Long Section

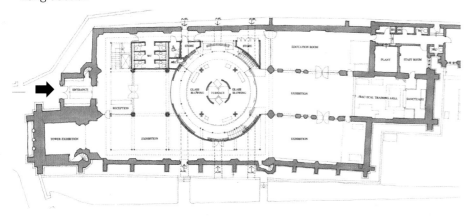

Ground Floor Plan

Temple Church, Bristol

We were commissioned by English Heritage at Temple Church, Bristol, to investigate the condition of the church, now roofless following fire-bombing in the Second World War, and to make recommendations for its future. We established that the decay of the church was escalating through being exposed to the weather on both sides, and that its long-term future was therefore at risk. We recommended that the church should be re-roofed, raising the question as to how this might best be done, and what use the building should then serve. Following discussion with Buro Happold, we proposed a lamella timber roof, sufficiently lightweight and rigid to sit on top of and to brace the decayed walls, with a pattern of lozenge-shaped compartments analogous to those on the lost medieval ceilings. As for use, we proposed a centre for glass-making, for which Bristol was once famous, to be run by Bristol Blue Glass, the only surviving glass-maker in Bristol. This would provide an attraction, a workshop, classes in glass-making and a cafe, all accessible to the public.

Our design for the internal interventions was stimulated by the archaeological discovery within the rectangle of the Hospitallers' church of the foundations of the circular Templar church which it replaced when the Templars were shut down and their wealth given to the Hospitallers. We placed a circular bottle kiln, such as might have been used in the 18th-century, at the centre of the Templar circle, with curved galleries around the perimeter. The enormous areas of window openings would have provided a magnificent opportunity for accommodating output from the workshop as a live project with public engagement. Sadly, capital grant funding was not forthcoming, and the project remains unrealised.

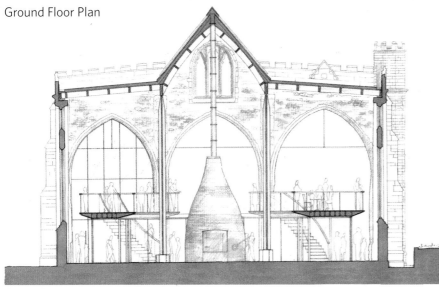

Cross Section

Whitechapel Art Gallery and Library

We were closely involved with the conversion of the former Whitechapel Library as an extension to the Whitechapel Art Gallery. Before the project started, we were commissioned by the Gallery to prepare a Conservation Plan in conjunction with Robert Thorne of Alan Baxter and Associates. This concluded that the best possible use for the building, giving that the library was definitely moving, was as an extension to the Gallery. Although stylistically very different, the two buildings were both built of terracotta within a few years of each other. The combined accommodation would allow exhibitions to be held in one building while the other was shut between shows – a major issue previously – and thus ensure a sustainable future for both buildings. The conversion was realised

brilliantly by Robbrecht en Daem working with Witherford Watson Mann and ourselves as conservation consultants. We advised on the integration of the two entrances and the library staircase, the necessity for a three-sided lift, and we achieved the restoration of the missing library gable, the pieces of which were found in store. We acted in our own right as architects for the repair of Harrison Townsend's wonderful Art Nouveau Gallery elevation. Its blank frieze panel has now finally been completed by Rachel Whiteread with gilded leaves that break free from the terracotta and surround four panels in raised relief, cast from the leaded light windows below. It is a remarkably successful exercise in contextualism.

Top
The Whitechapel Library *has been converted to act as an extension to the Whitechapel Art Gallery, Harrison Townsend's masterpiece. The terracotta gable has been reinstated and the blank frieze panel on the attic of the Gallery has been filled by Rachel Whiteread with gilded leaves that appear to have broken free from Townsend's towers.*

Top right
Finsbury Town Hall
*The Art Nouveau hall
of the 1890's Town Hall
now provides a fine dance
space for the Urdang
Academy of Dance, and
a source of funding from
functions.*

*Middle right
Dance class in the hall.*

*Bottom right
The wedding room looks
identical in its new location
on the opposite side of the
entrance.*

Finsbury Town Hall

Finsbury Town Hall, designed in 1890's with lavish
fin de siècle decoration, is one of those many town
halls made redundant following local government
reorganisation in 1974. Its primary function then
became as a Registry Office, until the Urdang
Academy of Dance offered to take on the whole
building in 2001, using the splendidly ornate first
floor hall as their main performance space. However,
they needed a second large dance studio, and, in
order to provide sufficient space, this required the
removal of the marriage room. There was an outcry
against the loss of the room, a fine panelled interior
of great significance to those who had been married
there. I was asked to advise on the heritage aspects
of the proposal, and whether there was some way
of meeting the objections. I realised that the room
to the left of the entrance was similar in scale to the
marriage room to the right of the entrance, and that
the windows were identical. I was therefore able to
satisfy all parties that the panelling could be taken
down and reconfigured to recreate a replica of the
marriage room. I doubt if many people notice the
difference. Dance classes now take place in a new
studio below the hall, or in the hall itself, which acts
as a vital income source for the Academy.

Top left
**London Dock,
Pennington Street
Warehouse**
*Each of the five areas was
open to the timber roof
trusses.*

Top right
*The vaults in their
Victorian heyday, filled
with barrels of wine and
spirits.*

Lower row
*The stone piers supporting
the vaults before, during
and after the building of
the cut-through.*

London Dock

Daniel Alexander, architect for the London Docks in 1805, is a particular hero of mine. As much as any, he founded the noble tradition of brick warehouses and factories of an elemental classical expression that became influential throughout Europe. They greatly impressed Schinkel, the great Prussian architect, when he visited England in 1826. Daniel Alexander is also likely to have been the architect for Clissold House, another building of primitive expression. It offers a remarkably early example of the Greek Revival, making use of the true Greek Doric Order sitting directly on the stylobate without a base.

We were determined to preserve this elemental quality in our conversion of the Pennington

Street warehouse, the only building of the London Dock to survive both WWII and the building of Murdoch's Fortress Wapping. We were also determined to avoid the prettification of the warehouses that had taken place in the Post-Modern conversion of Daniel Alexander's adjacent Tobacco Dock. The warehouse acted as the north wall of the London Dock and has massive brick walls designed to support a five-storey building. In fact only two were built, a single storey open to a pitched roof with wide-span timber trusses, and a basement storey with brick groin-vaulted cellars on stone columns stretching the whole 1000 foot length of the warehouse, subdivided into five areas with brick cross-walls. In these cellars a large proportion of the wine and liquor being imported into London

would have been stored in oak barrels.

Our aim was to make a cut through the centre of each area giving public access from Pennington Street to Quayside, the new road running between the warehouse and the large residential development by St George to the south. The cut-through extends to the full depth of the building, containing stairs and a lift leading to all levels, and flanked by full-height screens giving access to lettable units to each side. The stairs are detailed robustly with steel and glass, with balustrades of bronze-finished steel and stainless steel mesh, which is also used for the large sliding screens that close the cut-through at night. The cut-through is lit by large lantern lights above the retained timber trusses, allowing plentiful light to both levels.

The units to either side of the cut-throughs are also lit by large rooflights, and further cuts are made through the springing or the apex of the vaults to light the basement. These cuts have been carefully detailed to avoid the normal bland concrete ring-beam and to express instead the construction of the floor – brick-and-a-half arches, a concrete fill with exposed aggregate, and a concrete upstand below the screens and balustrades.

The lettable units have been left as shell-and-core for subsequent fit-out by the tenants. Current uses include a bar and architects' offices, but other uses, including a possible hotel, will follow. These will exploit the potential of the dramatic interior spaces of Daniel Alexander's sublime warehouse.

Top
The new lift shaft and staircase linking all levels via the central cut-through.

Lower row
The Pennington Street elevation before and after the insertion of new entrance gates and a glazed lantern.

Double page over
Large glazed screens fill each side of the cut-through, framing the stone columns, the brick vaults and the concrete fill.

Freston Tower

Freston Tower was built in the Tudor period overlooking the estuary of the River Orwell outside Ipswich, where the owner's ships would have off-loaded onto lighters. It was acquired by the Landmark Trust as a holiday home, taking advantage of the beautiful situation. The projecting stair turret rises a storey higher than the living room on the top floor, and gives access to a roof terrace with magnificent views over the estuary.

There were major technical challenges in converting a six storey tower with a single room open to the oak spiral staircase at each level. The solution was to provide a half-hour fire enclosure between the staircase and the kitchen, the main fire risk, and to introduce fire alarm-activated sprinklers at each floor level. The pipes are dry, and charged with water only when activated.

We gave much thought and debate to the treatment of the rendered window surrounds, intended to represent stone. Surprisingly, the pediments over the windows were un-rendered apart from the inside panels, which seem to float against the brick wall. Perhaps the classical language of the Renaissance was not well understood by the Tudor builders.

Top left
Freston Tower *seen from the north.*

Top right
Freston Tower acts as a welcoming beacon at dusk.

Opposite
The fictive stone architecture of the rendered window surrounds is belied by the un-rendered pediments.

Double page over
Freston Tower seen from the River Orwell.

CHAPTER FOURTEEN

The case for restoration

Restoration means the most total destruction which a building can suffer: a destruction out of which no remnants can be gathered. What copying can there be of surfaces that have been worn half an inch down? You may make a model of a building as of a corpse, but the old building is destroyed and that more totally and mercilessly than if it had sunk into a heap of dust, or melted into a mass of clay'.
Ruskin, *The Seven Lamps of Architecture,* 1849, The Lamp of Memory

Architecture is the masterly, correct and magnificent play of masses brought together in light.
Le Corbusier, *Vers une Architecture,* 1923

Restoration is something of a dirty word in this country, owing to the passionate views of Ruskin, William Morris and the Society for the Protection of Ancient Buildings. They identified the essence of a building as its substance or fabric, the materials of which it is made, the texture of age or decay, and in the pattern of alterations over time. But wherein, truly, lies the essence of a building? Is it in its substance and physical fabric, as held by Morris, or in its design and form, as held by Le Corbusier? The metaphysical relationship between substance and essence has exercised philosophers since Plato, Aristotle and Aquinas. However, a building is not a human being, and if it has a soul, its soul lives in the eyes and in the memory of man. Both the substance and the essence of a building are in its design, in its form, in its construction, and in all those qualities that make for Architecture, as well as in its fabric.

Opposite
Kenilworth Castle: *the restored Tudor Garden.*

I side with Plato rather than with Morris, and consider that it is possible to rebuild the fabric of a building lost to war, fire or disaster, and to regain its essence, so long as the evidence exists for its form, and that it is built with the same materials and techniques as the original; if so, then it will weather and acquire texture with age as did the original. Metaphysics relieves us of the feeling that such rebuilding is fake, pastiche or immoral. In the case of the Frauenkirche in Dresden, destroyed by bombing, or Mackintosh's Glasgow School of Art, destroyed by fire, the significance that can be regained vastly outweighs any significance that has been lost.

St Leonard's Shoreditch

The case for restoration of the galleries at St
Leonard's Shoreditch, designed by George Dance
the Elder in the 18th century and removed by
William Butterfield in the 19th century, was
compelling. A thorough study of the building
and of its condition revealed that the columns
of the nave, unbraced by galleries, were leaning
outwards and putting the church structurally at
risk. The restoration of the galleries, for which
good evidence existed in old photographs and
in other churches by Dance, would achieve
three things - the restoration of its Georgian
appearance as designed by Dance, a solution
to the structural problems, and the creation of
ancillary spaces below the galleries for lobbies
and vestries and meeting rooms. Unlike at
Christchurch Spitalfields, however, no attempt
was made to recreate the original rake at gallery
level, with its impossible sightlines. Instead, just
two rows of steeply raked seats were provided
with good sightlines, the remainder left as a flat
floor to allow flexible use.

Far left
St Leonard's, Shoreditch
*Drawing of the interior
with restored galleries and
a new stone floor.*

Top left
*The interior following
removal of George Dance
the Elder's galleries by
William Butterfield.*

Top right
*The interior of the church
following replacement of
the galleries.*

Bottom right
*There are only two lines of
benches on the galleries,
at a steeper pitch than the
original, in order to allow
better sightlines. The rest
of the gallery has a flat
floor to allow flexible use.*

Thorpe Coombe House, Walthamstow

Thorpe Coombe House, a Georgian villa in
Walthamstow, had, like Clissold House, been
derelict for many years, and was held together
by means of scaffolding below a temporary
roof. In this case restoration of the plan form
of the Georgian villa was essential for the
structural stability of the building, which had
been grievously altered. This involved much
detective work, for example in realising that the
bottom two sections of the staircase had been
inverted, so that the staircase turned through
90 rather 180 degrees. Reversion to the original
configuration allowed us to recreate its 18th
century appearance without loss of fabric. Old
photographs showed the Tuscan porch that had
been removed earlier this century. This evidence,
coupled with Georgian pattern books, allowed us
to restore the porch and the harmony of the front
elevation.

Left
Thorpe Coombe House
*The front of Thorpe Coombe House with
the Doric portico restored according to old
photos and Georgian pattern books.*

Top right
*The main ground floor front room and its
fine plaster ceiling have been restored to
their original splendour.*

Bottom right
*The staircase restored to its original
configuration.*

Kenilworth Castle Tudor Privy Garden

Much more controversial was our restoration for English Heritage of the Tudor Privy Garden at Kenilworth Castle, where Lord Leicester famously entertained Queen Elizabeth for 19 days in 1575. The garden, no doubt specially enhanced for the visit, survives only in a detailed description contained in a two-page letter of 1575 by Robert Langham. This describes a garden of four quarters arranged around a central fountain, overlooked from a terrace on the side of the castle keep, lined with obelisks, spheres and white bears, the emblem of Lord Leicester. Opposite the terrace was an aviary built against the castle wall. Despite extensive archaeological excavation, the only incontrovertible survival from the garden was the foundation of the fountain; otherwise the remains had been destroyed when the castle was slighted by Cromwell during the Civil War. However, at least this established the centre point for the setting out of the garden

For some of the elements of the garden the description was sufficiently detailed to allow a fairly precise restoration – for example the obelisks at the centre of the quarters, *upon a base two foot square a square pilaster rising pyramidically fifteen feet high, symmetrically pierced through from a foot beneath to two feet from the top.* A detailed

description of the fountain at the centre of the garden allowed a reconstruction by the Fairhaven Studio with an octagonal basin with panelled sides containing carved scenes from Ovid's metamorphoses, and *a column upright, in shape of two Atlants, joined together a back half, upholding a bowl three foot over.*

The aviary could be plausibly reconstructed from the letter, which describes the number and size of the great windows, the columns and entablature, even the jewels – diamonds, rubies, emeralds, sapphires - that decorated the frieze. Put together with the evidence provided by the porch on the side of the gatehouse, a reused outbuilding from the time of Lord Leicester and details of the classical orders given in Serlio's contemporary treatise, it proved possible to make a plausible reconstruction. In the case of the arbours, however, the letter contains no description; it is not even entirely clear whether the letter describes tunnel arbours at each end of the garden or pavilion arbours at each end of the terrace. We decided to build arbours at each end of the terrace based on the splendid contemporary arbour designed by du Cerceau for the garden at Montargis, for lack of any better home-grown example.

Previous double page
The Kenilworth Castle Tudor Garden *has been conjecturally recreated on the basis of a two-page letter of 1575 that gives a detailed written description of the garden.*

Top
The garden seen from the castle keep, with arbours at each end of the terrace, aviary against the castle wall and knots arranged around the central fountain.

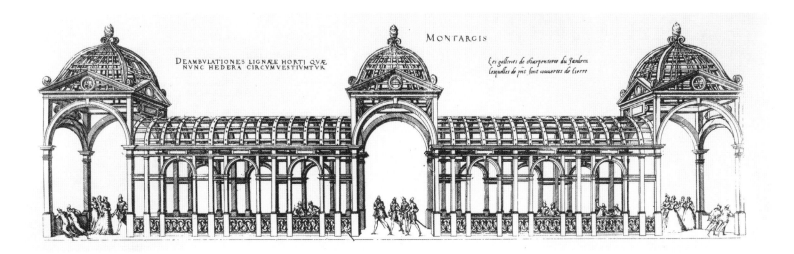

As architects tasked with realising the project on the ground, we worked closely with the expert panel to design and build the elements of the garden as authentically as possible. Notably, we used green oak for the steps, balustrades and superstructures of the aviary and arbours, working closely with Peter McCurdy and his excellent team of carpenters. The massive oak timbers were shaped and jointed using the tools and techniques available in the Tudor period, and as a result the structures will split and move, gaining interest and texture as they dry out. Only the need to comply with modern building regulations caused us to depart from authenticity through the addition of steel bracing bars to the aviary, and countersunk (and therefore invisible) steel flitch plates to the arbours.

The project represents the most ambitious attempt so far in this country to recreate the appearance of a Tudor garden. However, is *a lifeless forgery the sole result of all that wasted effort*, as Ruskin and Morris said about any attempt to restore the past? English Heritage justify it as an academic and scholarly reconstruction. The garden that it replaced was of no significance, built in the 1970's on the evidence of a print that is now known to be erroneous. The Tudor garden restoration is extremely popular with visitors, and the increased number of visitors enhances the economic sustainability of the site, one of English Heritage's top attractions. The recreation can reasonably claim to have restored a vivid sense of the garden visited by Langham in 1575, *whereby, at one moment, and in one place, at hand, without travel, to have so full fruition of so many God's blessings, by entire delight unto all senses at once.*

Top
The arbour at Montargis by du Cerceau 1560-1575 formed the basis for the design of the arbours.

Middle
The detailed description of the aviary, including details of its dimensions and its jewelled frieze, allowed a more reliable reconstruction of its design.

Bottom
The Tudor garden after painting of the aviary, obelisks and balustrade in imitation of the local pink sandstone.

Lupton Hall, Bedales School

By contrast, our restoration of Ernest Gimson's Lupton Hall at Bedales School, an Arts and Crafts masterpiece of 1911, was entirely uncontroversial. We removed the later accretions, including a theatre proscenium, to restore the hall to its original appearance as a specialist hall for music. Our only compromise was to drop the rake of the stage to become level, by lowering the rear edge of the stage as a single piece. The magnificent cruck-framed barn-like hall is now revealed in all its original splendour, making an inspiring setting for music-making and for concerts.

Upper
Bedales School
Lupton Hall at Bedales School, designed by Gimson in 1911, in its Edwardian heyday as school hall and auditorium.

Lower
Lupton Hall in its latter day use as a theatre.

Opposite
Lupton Hall repaired and restored to its original glory as a specialist hall for music, with the 'wondrous bee' reinstated in pride of place below the circular gable window.

CHAPTER FIFTEEN

Historic gardens and landscapes

I have always been interested in the context of historic buildings and their landscape setting, whether urban or rural. When designing new buildings in a historic setting, I have often considered that the external space, rather than the building, should be the primary space, and have avoided the modernist norm of a building sitting in space, in favour of a building or buildings surrounding space. In the context of the city, small enclosed spaces laid out with trees and planting can provide green lungs of extraordinary importance as a counterpart to buildings and hard landscape.

Opposite
Southwark Cathedral
The south churchyard offers two paths – a straight-through stone-paved path for busy commuters and a meandering perimeter gravel path with benches for visitors with time to stand and stare.

Bottom left
The Millennium Courtyard at Southwark Cathedral creates a new axial entrance to the Cathedral from the Thames Path, flanked by the refectory wing to the east and a raised planting bed for a line of liquidamber trees to the west.

Bottom right
The east churchyard reveals foundations of the Lady Chapel that was demolished for the building of John Rennie's London Bridge in 1824. It has a herb garden planted with medicinal herbs that were used in the monastic hospital that later became St Thomas's Hospital.

Southwark Cathedral Churchyard

Our new Millennium buildings at Southwark Cathedral were designed to surround the Millennium Courtyard, a three-sided courtyard that bears a memory of the monastic cloister that occupied the site before the Dissolution. Gates lead from a new entrance facing the river into the courtyard, flanked by the library and refectory to the east and a row of liquidamber trees on raised planting beds to the west, and thence to the new entrance on the axis of the north transept and tower. We also re-designed the north churchyard with two new paths running east-west, a fast straight-through path that leads from east and west to the main entrance into the Cathedral, and a slow meandering path that hugs the planting around the perimeter, lined with benches facing the Cathedral. This path is gently ramped to give equal access to the main entrance, circumventing the steps on the straight-through path. Finally we opened up the east churchyard as a quiet haven, overlooking raised planting beds aligned with the ruins of the Lady Chapel that were recovered by excavation. These are planted with herbs used in the hospital that was founded in the now demolished St Thomas' Chapel on the south side of the priory church.

Lambeth Palace Forecourt

Following completion of the courtyard project at Lambeth Palace we were asked to re-landscape the forecourt. Our design provides a broad paved driveway for vehicles approaching the Palace gatehouse, as well as paved paths for pedestrians. These are set in a sea of bonded gravel, similar to the landscaping and paving of Oxford and Cambridge college courts. The edge of the footpaths is marked by granite obelisks.

Queen's Chapel of the Savoy Churchyard

We were approached by the Duchy of Cornwall to mark their new development on the Strand by remodelling the churchyard of the Queen's Chapel of the Savoy, a Royal Peculiar. At first, we were asked to comment on the site of a proposed sculptural commission, but we pointed out that the vestry roofs were in a poor condition, and that the garden needed improvement in order to create a suitable site for a sculpture. The project then metamorphosed into something entirely different, concerned with re-roofing the vestries with copper roofs and re-landscaping the churchyard with a central level oval lawn surrounded by a sloping oval path. Level lawn and sloping path were both framed with stone borders, one flat, one sloping, touching on the centreline like armillary spheres. The sculptural commission ended up as an inscription around the level stone border.

Top
Lambeth Place
We redesigned the forecourt of Lambeth Palace as a hard landscape of gravel roadway and York stone-paved pedestrian paths.

Bottom
Savoy Chapel
The garden of the Savoy Chapel following the re-roofing of the vestries with copper roofing, and the re-design of the garden with an oval lawn with concentric oval stone borders.

Valentine's Park

Southwark Cathedral and the Savoy are in an urban setting, and a degree of formality in the design of the landscape seemed appropriate. By contrast, the setting at Valentine's Park in Redbridge was originally that of a Rococo garden to what, when built, was a rural mansion, and is now a historic house in a public park. We had earlier repaired the outside of the mansion and its remarkable embracing colonnaded wings, and had drawn up plans for the repair and restoration of the interior. We were then appointed to restore the Rococo garden with its extremely derelict but nonetheless splendid grotto, lake, walled garden and gardener's cottage. It proved an interesting challenge to repair the grotto, built of flint and rendered masonry, and to retain its rustic appearance over the underlying geometrical forms.

Simon Ablett held long discussions with Redbridge Council about the appropriate location for the café, whether in the house or in the grounds. At Clissold House it is in the house, and always has been; whether it would have gained listed building consent otherwise is a moot point, but I think there is great public benefit in being able to enjoy the historic house and landscape while eating and drinking. At Valentine's the house is a museum of itself and remains under-visited. Meanwhile, the café occupies the gardener's cottage overlooking the lovely walled garden, and has its own special charm.

Top
Valentines Park
The return to a state of nature of the Rococo garden at Valentine's Park had gone too far. We restored the remarkable long water with its rustic water source without destroying its picturesque charm.

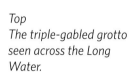

Top
The triple-gabled grotto seen across the Long Water.

Bottom
The inside of the walled garden, showing the attractive texture of new lime pointing to the historic brickwork of the grotto.

Top
The dovecote after repair.

Bottom
The new cafe in the gardener's cottage and walled garden.

CHAPTER SIXTEEN

The regeneration of historic areas

Through our work with the reuse of historic buildings we have become increasingly involved with the regeneration of historic areas. The issues are similar: how to make the circulation work for pedestrians, cyclists and vehicles, how to landscape the spaces between buildings, and how to make the most of the surviving old buildings in their relationship with the new. Conservation-led regeneration can harness the qualities of old buildings and the memory of the past for the benefit of present and future generations, and the reuse of old buildings can provide a distinctive sense of place that can only be acquired by new places through the passage of time.

King's Cross Regent Quarter

My first engagement with the regeneration of historic areas, as opposed to the conservation of individual buildings, came with my involvement as heritage adviser to P&O Developments in the redevelopment of three urban blocks on York Way to the east of King's Cross Station. These blocks had long been blighted by the threat of comprehensive development and by a road widening scheme for Caledonian Road that would have demolished several unlisted industrial buildings of the 1870's. These included in Block C (between Caledonian Road and Railway Street) the Pontifex Brass Works, a leadworks, a foundry and, in Block D to the north, stables for the London Omnibus Company, including a wonderful stepped ramp for horses leading to

further stables on the first floor. These buildings were characterised by heavy brick walls, open-joisted floors and slate roofs, supported by roof trusses consisting of massive timber compression members and iron rod tension members, of exceptional interest. For the previous ten or fifteen years the buildings had been occupied by short-term tenants, of which the Jaguar repair workshop in No 34B York Way, with the best of the Victorian roof structures, was the most evocative, strewn with walnut dashboards, eviscerated electrics strung over the ties of the roof trusses, spray paint graffiti on the walls, and, best of all, a staircase shaft to the rear filled with the dismembered limbs and torsos of mannequins, reminiscent of Jack the Ripper.

Opposite
King's Cross Regent Quarter: *No 34B York Way following repair and conversion to Impact Hub for co-workers, revealing the magnificent hipped roof with timber compression members and iron tension members.*

Bottom left
No 34B York Way during its atmospheric short-life use as a Jaguar car repair workshop.

Bottom right
Pontifex Brassworks at No 32 York Way in its heyday.

Ironically my first engagement was to advise P&O Developments on the contextual design of a new hotel building that would have replaced the Pontifex Brass Works. However, the Islington Society protested against the demolition of the unlisted buildings in the Conservation Area, and at a remarkable planning committee meeting fifteen articulate local objectors spoke against the proposals, and for an alternative conservation-led regeneration of the site. The application, despite officers' recommendation for approval, was deferred pending the submission of reconsidered proposals. As a result, P&O appointed an entirely new team to devise a new masterplan for the site. I was sounded out by a Director of P&O over lunch at his table at the RAC Club, and invited to join RHWL Architects as heritage consultant. At our first meeting, I presented the proposals that I had prepared, speculatively, when first appointed. These showed how the conservation and retention of the Victorian industrial buildings was compatible with the creation of a new hotel and a new office block in the centre of the site, as required by P&O to ensure the commercial viability of the development. The proposals were dependent on the abandonment of an old road widening scheme, which released enough land for the new hotel without requiring the demolition of the Pontifex Brass Works. The other key aspect of the proposal was the creation of a new north-south route through the interiors of all three urban blocks, giving independent access to the buildings in the interior of the blocks,

where previously the east-west boundaries of the industrial units had been impenetrable. The proposal formed the basis for the regeneration of the blocks, with the exception of the major new office block in the interior of Block C, for which P&O required an entrance that announced itself from York Way. Given that access to the interior of the site at this point was blocked by the Jahn building, another fine Victorian industrial building with a long raised roof lantern, this was initially problematic. However, some detective work comparing an 1891 Insurance plan and a plan of 1900 revealed that the Jahn building had originally been built shorter, with an open courtyard facing York Way that contained a chimney. The chimney had been swallowed up when the Jahn building was extended shortly after construction, as was proved when evidence of the earlier end wall was uncovered following the demolition of the extension to create the new office entrance. The restoration of the forecourt, and the revealing of the tall brick chimney, now provide a handsome entrance to the new office block behind.

Next door, 34B York Way, the former Jaguar repair workshop with the finest of the Victorian roof structures, is now Impact Hub, a co-working space. The area has been re-branded as the Regent Quarter, and the prostitutes, for whom the area was previously renowned, have moved on.

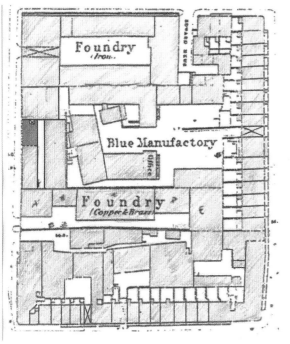

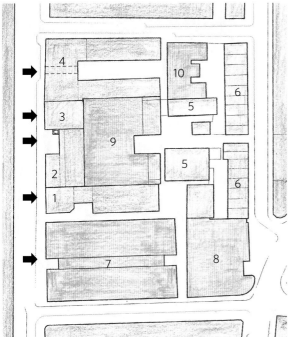

King's Cross Lighthouse Block

Following the realisation of the new masterplan for block C to the north of Pentonville Road, I was invited by P&O Developments to take over the design of the Lighthouse building to the south, with its distinctive turret on the sharp angle where Pentonville Road and Gray's Inn Road divide. The block on which it sits is characterised by the distinctive lighthouse turret on top of the listed building at the west end of the block, facing towards King's Cross Station, flanking buildings of four or three storeys and attic, stepping down in scale towards the single storey shops to the east. The whole building sits above the tracks of the 1850's Metropolitan Railway, which was of course inviolable.

The only way to achieve P&O's aim of creating modern offices on the site was to remove all the cross-walls and chimney breasts that took up a significant proportion of the internal area, and to make a virtue of façade retention. Michael Asselmeyer and I did this by raising the internal floor levels to sill level of the windows, allowing a greater ceiling height in the ground floor bar and restaurant. This gave an elemental trabeated expression to the window surrounds on the upper floors, inspired by Schinkel, within masonry elevations that we extended round the whole perimeter of the building. Within this masonry envelope, we extended the new steel structure above roof level, expressed as a steel and glass pavilion reminiscent of Mies van der Rohe's IIT buildings.

The previous scheme had a lift and stair core to the east, with long fire-rated corridors to provide means of escape from each floor. We improved on this by designing a new spiral escape stair extending the lighthouse turret down to ground level within a cylindrical shaft of glass bricks. This would have glowed at night as a beacon visible from the whole length of Euston Road.

Sadly, our designs proved too adventurous for the Camden planner who sat on the plans and refused to determine the application until P&O offered a watered-down version of the same proposal with traditional dormers and slate roof. They later sold the site, which has been developed by others under a lumpen new roof.

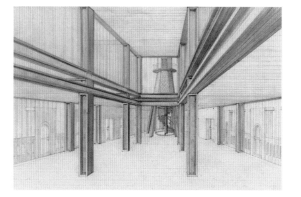

Top right
Lighthouse Block, King's Cross *in its state of dereliction.*

Top left
View of the Lighthouse with the new attic floor behind.

Middle left
Our scheme placed a new Miesian steel building inside the masonry shell of the Lighthouse Block, part façade retention, part elemental trabeated extension.

Bottom
View from the top floor office towards the Lighthouse.

Oxford Castle

We were appointed by Trevor Osborne to act as heritage consultants for the regeneration of the Oxford Castle and Prison to create a new quarter for Oxford with shops, bars, flats and a hotel. The development has opened up a formerly totally closed site; and it has proved remarkably successful in creating new public spaces for people and a complementary range of beneficial and viable uses. It is a startling demonstration of the possibilities of heritage-led regeneration.

The Victorian wing of the prison had fearsome walls with high-level windows, lighting the stone-vaulted cells inside. The conversion to hotel use was effected by removing the cross walls between cells to form hotel bedrooms of two or three bays with a one bay ensuite bathroom. The major design issue was how to give the rooms an external aspect and view without compromising the stern elevations. Rather than dropping the stones of the stringcourse where a window was required, we retained the stringcourse intact and punched new smaller windows below, set flush with the outside face of the wall. As only one window in every three or four needed to be dropped, and since these dropped windows could be paired symmetrically, their impact on the external elevations is remarkably small.

The site of Oxford Prison is that of the original Norman castle, of which the castle mound and other Norman features survive. There is also St George's Tower, which is thought to be of Saxon origin. We conserved the scheduled Ancient Monument using the lightest possible touch in repairing it fabric, making it publicly accessible and adding a new viewing platform on the roof, giving a panoramic view of the tower and spires of Oxford.

Top
Oxford Castle
Our viewing platform on the roof of St George's Tower gives the best view of the towers and spires of Oxford.

Middle
View of the Victorian wing after conversion to hotel use. Rather than drop the stones of the heavy stringcourse, flush glazed windows were inserted where needed below the stringcourse to give external views to the hotel rooms.

Bottom
Detail of the new dropped windows below the stringcourse.

Lancaster Canal Quarter

SAVE, the highly effective campaigning organisation formed by Marcus Binney, had launched a campaign to prevent a retail-led development on the site of the Lancaster Canal Quarter that would have destroyed most of the surviving unlisted 19th century buildings in the Conservation Area. A new bridge would have led from the town-centre to a new shopping mall on the land rising towards the canal at the top of the site to the east, obliterating all the Victorian shops on the 'nose' of the site facing towards the town centre.

I was asked to prepare an alternative vision for the site that would retain the two theatres, the unlisted brewery building, and all the buildings on the 'nose', as the focus for a conservation-led development of the site. There was plenty of space for new development without destroying the Conservation Area and its characterful buildings, and I presented my proposals at a public meeting in Lancaster, attended by many concerned locals. At the end of the meeting Marcus Binney asked for a show of hands as to which proposal found greater favour with those present. All but two preferred my scheme; the council member present and the representative of the developers chose not to express their preference.

It therefore came as a surprise to me some while later to receive a call from Chapman Taylor, asking me to join them as heritage consultant to prepare a new scheme for Canal Corridor site. I told them of my earlier involvement with SAVE, they told British Land, the developer, and I was impressed that they nevertheless chose to appoint me. Together we devised a new scheme that retained the significant buildings, creating a mix of small and large scale shop units, and converted the derelict brewery buildings, into an arts centre. The scheme would have provided a vibrant mix of arts, theatre, retail, leisure, bar and restaurant uses. The project remains as yet

unrealised. It would be a pleasing irony if the most appropriate form of development turned out to be small scale, incremental regenerative reuse after all.

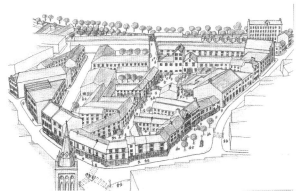

Opposite page
St George's Tower at Oxford Castle, *a defensive tower of Saxon origin, now forms the heart of the visitor experience with a viewing platform on the roof.*

Top
Lancaster Canal Corridor
The derelict brewery in the middle of the site.

Middle
Our alternative sketch scheme for the Lancaster Canal Corridor was commissioned by SAVE to show how all the interesting surviving 19th century buildings could be reused in an incremental, conservation-led regeneration of the site.

Bottom
We made the case for the special qualities of the brewery building and proposed its conversion as an arts centre. The brewery was subsequently listed.

CHAPTER SEVENTEEN

Conservation cause célèbre: St Pancras

Too beautiful and romantic to survive.
Sir John Betjeman

I remember it as a rat-infested dump. Water dripped down walls. Wires hung from ceilings. Pigeons colonised turrets and rafters. Gormenghast could not do justice to the profile of that destitute old lady, slumped at the far end of Euston Road. Poor St Pancras hotel embodied the contempt of modernism for anything old, stylish, romantic and, above all, Victorian.
Simon Jenkins, *The Guardian*, 8 July 2011, *Sir George Gilbert Scott, the unsung hero of British architecture.*

The saving of St Pancras Station and Chambers and their conversion to international station and hotel must rank as the greatest conservation success story of the century. Built by Sir George Gilbert Scott from 1870-76 in conjunction with Barlow's St Pancras Station, it was the last of the railway termini to reach London, and accordingly Scott had the budget to design what he liked, and the opportunity to demonstrate that Gothic was as effective a style for secular buildings as for ecclesiastical. Indeed, Scott's Gothic was able to negotiate the oblique line of Midland Road and the constraints of a station at first floor level with taxi ramps and drop-off, all in a picturesque composition of towers, turrets and arcades. I am convinced that Scott set out to demonstrate how Venetian Gothic, extolled in Ruskin's Stones of Venice, could be made applicable to a commercial building, with its elevational parti based on the Doge's Palace and its Venetian Gothic screen in the western entrance.

Opposite
St Pancras Hotel
View of the restored St Pancras Hotel from Euston Road with the new wing of 170 hotel bedrooms facing Midland Road on the left.

Though a Grand Hotel, it was not in the grandest part of town, and technological developments put it progressively in the shade: when built it only had eight bathrooms. The hotel closed in 1933 and was partly fitted out as offices for British Rail, an adaptation that inserted suspended ceilings in all the main rooms, above which the mutilated original ceilings survived. The station was saved by reason of its listing and the campaign by the Victorian Society, with the support of Sir John Betjeman, whose statue appropriately now graces the station concourse. Its real salvation only came with the decision to make St Pancras station the London terminus for Eurostar trains from the continent, with the continental trains using Barlow's trainshed. Arrivals and departures, together with the public concourse, are situated in the undercroft below.

Working with RHWL Architects in 1997 we became conservation members of the team that took on the project for the conversion of St Pancras Chambers, as it was then known, into a grand hotel and residential apartments. However, design only really started ten years later when the international terminus was sufficiently far advanced. By this time, the original developers had fallen away, leaving Manhattan Lofts, under the remarkable Harry Handelsman, to carry the whole of a massively complicated project.

It had always been apparent that the re-establishment of a grand hotel at St Pancras would be dependent on the provision of 170 additional bedrooms in a new wing, and allowance had been made in the design of St Pancras International Station for new foundations to support a seven storey building parallel to the train shed on its western side. But it soon became clear that English Heritage (now Historic England) had severe reservations about the emerging design, then based on the analogy of two trains (of hotel rooms) entering a glass trainshed. Geoff Mann of RHWL then turned to us to devise a solution with which English Heritage might be satisfied.

It was clear that what they wanted was a design that was better related to its context, and reflected the red brick Gothic of Scott's hotel, without being too literal. So we started with an analysis of the design and building of the station and of the hotel, noting the curved wall on the east side of the station and the way in which the tall rooms of the main south elevation are subdivided by a mezzanine where the building turns the corner into Midland Road. We also noted how the oblique wall to Midland Road at ground level, originally only a single storey high, had been progressively extended to a second storey later on. This had been demolished for the building of St Pancras International station, and rebuilt with the complete ground floor arcade as before, but with a second floor only in the position of the energy centre for the station. Our first decision was to extend the first floor arcade to accommodate two floors of hotel rooms facing Midland Road: this allowed the removal of one floor of the proposed seven storey block of new hotel rooms. A further floor of the west elevation was (visually) removed by combining two levels of hotel rooms within a single arch, and two further floors were removed from the elevation by placing them within a pitched roof, as found on the original building. By these expedients, a seven storey elevation was reduced to a three storey elevation and Historic England were content.

Elevation to Midland Road

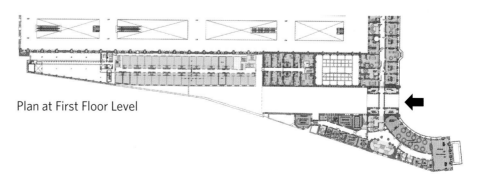

Plan at First Floor Level

Left top
St Pancras Hotel
The end elevation of the new wing has stepped gables, a stripped-down version of Scott's.

Left middle
The tower and entrance concourse seen from the terrace outside the new wing.

Left bottom
Plan of St Pancras Station and Hotel and the new elevation to Midland Road.

Right
View of the elevational parti of Scott's hotel with its successive orders of round arch-headed windows, pointed arch-headed windows and triple lancet windows surmounted by a double height roof with dormers and tall chimneys.

Far right
Drawing of our elevational parti for the new wing, with its successive orders of round-arched arcades, two levels of rooms within a single pointed arch, triple lancet windows and two floors in the attic. The unmoulded brickwork of the window reveals is nowhere more than one brick thick.

Working with Richard Hill, we developed an articulation to our brickwork distinctly different from Scott's. The brick arches are undecorated and unmoulded apart from a simple stringcourse at the springing of the arches. Our approach has analogies with Philip Webb's stripped-down Gothic at William Morris's Red House and at Standen; it is also influenced by St Albans Abbey, where the arches of the Norman nave have unmoulded planes of recession based on the size of a Roman brick, identical to those in our new wing at St Pancras. In fact, our new brick elevation is nowhere more than one brick thick, as the foundations would not take any greater load. It is nevertheless self-supporting and only braced by the steelwork behind. Remarkably, we were able to avoid any expansion joints because the bricks are all laid in lime mortar.

Elsewhere, our input was mainly in the design of the public areas of the hotel, and followed the geometry, materials and colours of the original building, albeit without the decorative detail – a stripped down language of detailing.

The main entrance posed a formidable challenge in view of the slope of the former taxi rank. We intended to place the entrance doors below the bridge under the large tower arch at an intermediate level between outside and inside, with steps on either side and an access ramp under the side arch. This was modified on the advice of the Council's access officer to a ramp leading to the entrance lobby from outside and steps inside. These were carefully cut away to reveal the bases of the Scott's piers, a detail borrowed from Carlo Scarpa.

The screens that enclose the entrance concourse of the hotel, formerly the taxi rank, follow the geometry of the glazed roof, are painted Midland red, and are supported by lattice beams painted sky blue like the roof trusses. The floor of the concourse is paved with woodblock flooring flanked by pavements of York stone with granite kerbs, a memory of the taxi rank. In the platform level rooms on the Euston Road frontage a remarkable level of survival of original fabric was uncovered behind the casings and above the ceilings of the 20th century station and retail fit-out. It proved possible to retain the full height of the rooms in the corridors and in the semicircular staircase, which was restored to its original appearance.

Crick Smith carried out architectural paint research by means of paint sections and scrapes, allowing the full history of decoration of the hotel rooms to be reconstructed. As part of the listed building consent conditions, five historic areas had to be redecorated in an appropriate historical colour scheme, namely the sequence of spaces leading from the west portico entrance, along the ground floor corridor, up the main stair to the first floor corridor and thence to the ladies' smoking room. This could be done from the scrapes and research in all areas, but Historic England insisted on the retention of the later Edwardian fleur-de-lys pattern in the staircase in view of what they called its iconic status in published views of the grand staircase.

Opposite
The entrance concourse is laid out as two stone pavements with a field of woodblock, echoing the former taxi rank. The screens which enclose and subdivide the space are supported by cantilevered lattice beams painted in the station livery of Midland red and light blue.

Top left
The original main entrance was rediscovered behind later casings, and reinstated as the premier lounge of the hotel, restoring the truncated semi-circular stair that leads to the hotel suites on the first floor.

Top middle
View along the first floor corridor before work started.

Top right
The boiler in the derelict building.

Left above
The new entrance screen and lobby below the tower.

Left below
New steps leading from the entrance to the concourse.

Opposite
George Gilbert Scott's famous staircase with its later fleur-de-lys decoration and carpet restored.

Top row left
A window was cut through to link the concourse with the new lift lobby and the original main staircase beyond.

Top row right
The new lift lobby with stainless steel mesh balustrades matching those used to protect the historic staircases.

Middle row left
The booking office bar.

Middle row right
The restaurant with its restored plasterwork and decoration.

Bottom row left
The former main entrance to the hotel has been restored as a bar for the restaurant in the curved wing.

Bottom row right
The magnificent ladies' smoking room on the first floor is the culmination of the historic sequence leading from the western entrance via the main staircase.

The engineering required to achieve the conversion was heroic. The foundations had been designed to carry a building parallel to the train shed, not on the oblique line of Midland Road: our two mezzanine levels of hotel rooms are therefore hung from massive beams cantilevered from the main building. Moreover, the main hotel building has to span the 40 metre width of the loading bay of the railway without intermediate support. The elevation therefore screens a two storey triangulated steel truss, and the virtue of the Gothic arches becomes apparent in allowing full height glazing in the arched windows that fits tangentially between the diagonal members of the steel trusses.

The services engineering was similarly heroic, with the whole of the fourth floor corridor sacrificed to providing horizontal service runs from the main plant room in the roof of Barlow House. All the pipework was carefully fitted between the members of the trusses. The vertical risers were accommodated in linenfold panelled casing in the corridors, following the pattern used by Scott, but the new bathroom drainage could not run through the basement (which was reserved for the railway), and had to run at ceiling level in the platform rooms. We nevertheless managed to keep the pipework out of the restored corridor and the original entrance hall, which we could restore to full height.

We were happy to have been involved in such a fascinating project. The conversion to hotel and apartments works supremely well, and is a perfect fit for the building. It is quite remarkable that the whole restoration and conversion of the listed building should have been achieved without any public subsidy, and I am full of admiration for Harry Handelsman's nerve in seeing it through when the other partners backed out.

Top
The Midland Road wing under construction. The new wing acts as a bridge over the 30m wide loading bay by means of a two-storey lattice truss. The mezzanine level rooms on the street façade are hung from cantilevered beams.

Bottom
View of the new wing with is gentle curve towards Midland Road. The arched windows are tangential to the triangulated steel truss which is hidden behind the brickwork.

St Pancras Station

During the planning of the hotel project, I was consulted by London and Continental Railways about a serious problem that they had with the design of the retail units in the lower level concourse of St Pancras Station. The railway development had been approved by Act of Parliament, and included a Heritage Deed requiring, among other things, that the shopfronts on the west side of the main north-south concourse be located behind the face of the original brick piers. However, because of the oblique line of Midland Road, most of the shop units would have been restricted to a single bay, and therefore commercially useless. I devised the strategy of bringing fully glazed shopfronts forward of the columns, symmetrical with the new shopfronts to the east, but setting them back to the brickwork in four positions along the length, so as to read as bay windows rather than as a continuous glass frontage. Because the glazing is recessed and in shadow the brickwork now reads as an attractive backdrop to the shops and bars lining the concourse.

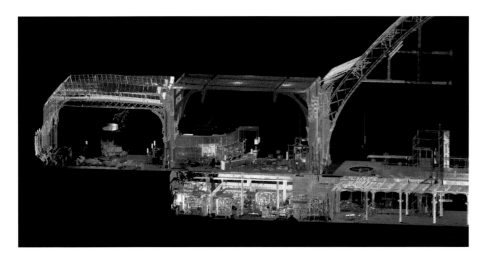

Top
St Pancras Station
This laser point-cloud survey shows the intimate connection between the Scott's hotel concourse to the left, Scott's booking office bar in the middle, and Barlow's station and undercroft to the right.

Bottom
The lower concourse of St Pancras Station with the line of the new glazed shopfronts set forward of the flanking brick walls of the station. The line of the brickwork is retained on the cross-axes, leading to taxis and washrooms, and providing space for flower stalls.

CHAPTER EIGHTEEN

Old buildings, new architecture

Just to stretch out on the grass, as you used to do.
Good to touch, good to feel.
Things that cost nothing, that everyone has,
That mean so much; these things are real.
Ramuz/Stravinsky, *The Soldier's Tale,* translated by Michael Flanders and Kitty Black

Opposite
Clissold Park
Weekend crowds enjoying the arcadian landscape and café at Clissold Park.

Time past and time future
What might have been and what has been
Point to one end, which is always present.
TS Eliot, *Four Quartets*, Burnt Norton

Bottom left
Just what is it that makes today's homes so different, so appealing?
Richard Hamilton, poster for This is Tomorrow, Whitechapel Art Gallery 1956.

Just what is it that makes working with old buildings so different, so appealing? For a start, there is the opportunity to work with beautiful natural materials – stone, brick, oak, lead, wrought iron, brass, gold leaf. Then there is the ability to make the case for construction and detailing that avoids the commercial exigencies that govern most contemporary projects, thanks to the carrot of grant aid and the stick of listed building consent. There is the heady possibility that what you have designed may still be around in 500 years' time. But most importantly there is the opportunity to add a new layer of architecture and history to the layers that are already present, allowing the past to serve and enrich the present and the future for the benefit of all.

Middle left
Community consultation at Toynbee Hall.

A feeling for the continuity of past, present and future, so strongly evoked by TS Eliot, gives meaning to our work with old buildings, based on the memory and significance that buildings and places have for people, and which forge their sense of identity. The role that our buildings can have in everyday life – and we are fortunate that most of the buildings on which we have worked are in public ownership – is the richest reward for our work, whether attending evensong at Southwark or at St Albans Abbey, helping others to discover the fascination of Sutton House, or watching the crowds at Clissold House on a sunny weekend.

Middle
Looking up the Tudor chimney at Eastbury Manor.

Middle right
Looking below the floorboards at Sutton House.

Conservation in the context of old buildings is ultimately a matter of sustainability, handing down our legacy of old buildings to future generations in good repair, equipped to fulfil a beneficial role today and in the future. However, it is also a matter of Architecture, and I have shown how the creation of architectural quality in repair, alteration and new building in an historic context is central to our work, and to our appreciation of the role that old buildings can play in everyday life. Working with old buildings is as rich a canvas for architectural endeavour as working with new buildings, and one of equally enduring value.

Bottom right
Eastbury Manor welcoming at night.

Projects and Clients

1986 CHAPTER 1
The Old Dispensary, Stratford
Timber-framed Georgian house
Repair and conversion to offices
LB Newham Museum Service

1987
Sutton Place, Guildford
Tudor prodigy house
Restoration of the terracotta elevations
The Sutton Place Foundation

1987 to date CHAPTER 1
Ragged School Museum, Limehouse
Victorian warehouse/ Ragged School
Conversion to museum use
Ragged School Museum Trust

1989 to date CHAPTER 2, 11
Sutton House, Hackney
Tudor house 1535 for Sir Ralph Sadleir
Restoration for heritage/community use
The National Trust

1991 to date CHAPTER 5, 11
Eastbury Manor, Barking
Tudor merchant's house of 1570
Restoration for heritage/community use
LB Barking and Dagenham/ NT/HLF

1993
Hayes Road, Bromley
Victorian house
Conservatory/dining extension
Private client

1994 CHAPTER 14
Thorpe Coombe House, Walthamstow
Derelict Georgian villa
Conversion to head office use
Heritage of London Trust / HLF

168

1994 CHAPTER 10
Blackfriars, Gloucester
Medieval Priory/Regency houses
Restoration and re-roofing
English Heritage

1995 CHAPTER 12
Jesus College, Cambridge
C14 hall with 1703 panelling
Redecoration, new servery and lighting
Master and Fellows of Jesus College

1995
Tudor Hall, Barnet
Tudor Hall of brick and oak
Conversion for college common room
Barnet College

1995
St Ethelburga, Bishopsgate
Medieval church bombed by the IRA
Rebuilding with new building to rear
Friends of St Ethelburga

1995
Rainham Hall, Essex
Early Georgian merchant's house
Reroofing and upgrading
The National Trust

1996
City of London churches
All 37 churches in the City of London
Survey of condition and uses
English Heritage/Alan Baxter

1996
Inchmery House, Hampshire
19th century house on the Solent
Major remodelling
Private client

1996
Ashton Court, Bristol
Grade 1 Stuart and later house
Development study
Bristol City Council

1996
St George's Gardens, Bloomsbury
Georgian burial ground
Restoration and public access
London Borough of Camden/ HLF

1996 to 2015 CHAPTER 14
St Leonard's, Shoreditch
Georgian church by Dance the Elder
Repairs and restoration of galleries
St Leonard's PCC/HLF

1996 CHAPTER 10
St Luke's, Kentish Town
Church by Basil Champneys 1867
Major structural and external repairs
Churches Conservation Trust

1997
Oxney Court, Kent
Picturesque villa of 1820
Consent for rebuilding from ruin
Private client

1997 to 2014 CHAPTER 3, 11, 15
Southwark Cathedral
C13 Priory, Victorian restoration
Millennium project, reordering
Dean and Chapter/Millennium Lottery

169

2002 CHAPTER 13
Freston Tower, Suffolk
Tudor brick lookout tower
Repair and conversion for holiday use
The Landmark Trust

2002
Lincoln Cathedral
Medieval cathedral
Study of development options
The Dean and Chapter

2002 CHAPTER 4
Burghley House, Stamford
Elizabethan house and C18 brewhouse
New visitor building and exhibition
Burghley House Preservation Trust

2002 CHAPTER 13
Whitechapel Library
Former library in the Jewish East End
Consultancy/repair of Gallery facade
Whitechapel Art Gallery

2002
Peterhouse, Cambridge
Rear Court overlooking Coe Fen
Competition for new student rooms
The Master and Fellows

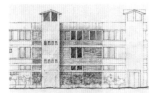

2003
The Houses of Parliament
Barry and Pugin 1830 – 1870
Study of flat roofs
Parliamentary Estates

2003
8 Guilford Street
Georgian house
Conversion to lecture room and offices
NADFAS

2004 CHAPTER 13
Finsbury Town Hall
High Victorian Town Hall
Advice on conversion to dance school
Urdang Academy of Dance

2004 CHAPTER 10
The Garrick Club
Italianate palazzo
Cleaning and repair of front elevation
The Garrick Club

2005 CHAPTER 8
St Paul's, Hammersmith
C19 Gothic church by Vulliamy
New western extension
St Paul's PCC

2005 CHAPTER 12
Russian Orthodox Cathedral
Vulliamy, Harrison Townsend
Internal redecoration and relighting
The Russian Orthodox Cathedral

2006 CHAPTER 17
St Pancras Station
1870's by Barlow and Ordish
Design consultancy for shopfronts
London and Continental Railways

2006 CHAPTER 9, 11
Kenilworth Castle, Warwickshire
One of England's foremost castle sites
New visitor building, Tudor Garden
English Heritage

2006
Brockwell Hall, Herne Hill
Georgian house in public park
Feasibility study for reuse of the house
London Borough of Lambeth

2006
Hampstead Churchyard
Georgian churchyard
Restoration with improved landscaping
Hampstead Church PCC/HLF

2007
Bishopsgate Institute
Harrison Townsend 1895
Conservation Plan
The Bishopsgate Institute

2007
Holburne Museum, Bath
Museum in former Georgian house
Listed building consultancy
Eric Parry Architects

2007
Stoke Newington
Triangular site in Victorian street
New courtyard house
Private Client

2008
Eastgate House, Rochester
Tudor townhouse
Study for conversion to community use
Medway Council

2009
Grafton Street
Georgian house by Sir Robert Taylor
Restoration as private house
Private client

2010 CHAPTER 10
King's Cross Granary Building
Warehouse building by Lewis Cubitt
Repair of the exterior
Central St Martins/ Stanton Williams

2008 CHAPTER 5
Clissold House, Stoke Newington
Late Georgian villa in public park
Conversion to cafe and community uses
London Borough of Hackney/HLF

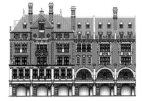

St Albans Abbey 2000-2018
RIBA National Award 2018

Awards

Burghley House, Stamford
LABC Award for Best Commercial Project 2006

Brighton College
RIBA South Award Shortlist 2017
RIBA South Award for Cairn's Tower, 2017
Civic Trust Awards Regional Finalist 2016

Clissold House, Hackney
RIBA London Award Shortlist 2012
Hackney Design Award 2012

Dagenham Civic Centre
Green Apple Awards Nomination 2005

Freston Tower, Suffolk
Civic Trust Award Commendation 2005
RIBA Conservation Commendation 2005

Fulham Island
Building for Life Silver Commendation 2001

Kenilworth Castle
Warwick District Council Design Award 2006
Civic Trust Awards Special Mention 2007
The Wood Awards Highly Commended 2006

King's Cross Central St Martins
RIBA Award 2012

King's Cross Regent Quarter
Islington Society Award for Architecture and Conservation 2006

Lambeth Palace Courtyard and Crypt
RFAC Building of the Year Shortlist 2001
Civic Trust Awards Commendation 2002

Oxford Castle
RICS Awards Project of the Year 2007
RIBA South Award 2007
Civic Trust Outstanding Centre Vision Award
Best Hotel & Leisure Project Award 2007
RICS South East Best Regeneration Scheme 2007
Mail on Sunday Mixed Use Development 2007
MIPIM Best Hotel and Leisure Project 2007
Oxford Preservation Trust Award 2007

Rawstorne Place, The Barn
LB Islington Award for Good Conservation

30 Romford Road, E15
Civic Trust Awards Commendation 1989
Mansell Refurbishment Commendation 1989
London Electricity Energy Efficiency Award 1989

Southwark Cathedral Millennium Project
RIBA Award 2002
ADAPT Trust Access Award Shortlist 2002
Civic Trust Awards Commendation 2002
Stone Federation Awards Commendation 2002
Tylers and Bricklayers Special Award 2002
Architectural Ironmongers Guild Award 2003
National Stone Craft Awards Commendation 2003
Landscape Institute 75th Anniversary Award 2003

St Albans Abbey
RIBA National Award 2017
RIBA East Award 2017
RIBA East Conservation Award 2017
RIBA East Project Architect of the Year Award 2017
St Albans Civic Society Award 2010
Hertfordshire Design Awards Special Conservation Award 2018

St Pancras Hotel
RIBA Award 2012
RIBA London and English Heritage Best Building in a Historic Context 2012
BDA Awards Best Architectural Achievement 2012
Brick Awards Best Refurbishment Finalist 2011
European Hospitality Awards Hotel of the Year 2012
Tylers & Bricklayers Award Commendation 2012
LPA Historic Building Management Award 2012
LABC Best Commercial Development 2012
RIBA London Conservation Award list 2012

St Paul's Church, Hammersmith
RIBA Award 2012

Sutton House, Hackney
Civic Trust Award 1996
Europa Nostra Award 1995
Interpret Britain Award 1995

Valentine's Park, LB Redbridge
Georgian Group Award 2010
Landscape Institute Commendation 2010
Georgian Group Award for the Restoration of a Georgian Garden or Landscape 2010

Articles

Brighton College
Building Design Online, *Victorian tower extension*, Amanda Birch, Jan 2015
RIBA Journal, *Patience Rewarded*, Hugh Pearman, Feb 2015

Burghley Brewhouse
Architects' Journal, *Critic's Choice*, Andrew Mead, June 2006
Historic House magazine, *Burghley's evolution*, Autumn 2006

Christ Church Hampstead
Church Building Magazine, March/April 2017

Dagenham Civic Centre
Architecture Today, *Civic Star,* issue 147, 2003

Eastbury Manor
Building Design, *Mild Manored*, Jonathan Foyle, 30 May 2003

Freston Tower
AJ Specification, *Brickwork repairs*, 2005

Jesus College, Cambridge
Building Design, *Back to Baroque in College Hall*, 26 Jan 1996

Kenilworth Castle Garden
Building Design, Graham Bizley, 24 Oct 2008
ASCHB Transactions, *The recreation of the Elizabethan Privy Garden at Kenilworth Castle*, Richard Griffiths, 2010
Heritage Today, *Flight of fancy*, Oct 2008

King's Cross Granary Building
Building Design Magazine, *Like a cork to an enormous bottle,* Oct 2011

Lambeth Palace Courtyard Project
Building Design, *Divine intervention,* Kieran Long, 16 June 2000
Church Building Magazine, Simon Ablett, Jul/Aug 2000
Building Design Features, 2002
English Heritage, *Capital Solutions,* 2004

Methodist Central Hall, Westminster
Building Design, *Solutions: how we cracked it*, 1 Dec 2006
Church Building Magazine, 2006
Church Building Magazine, *Chapel revamp,* 2004

NADFAS, 8 Guildford Street
NADFAS Review, Summer 2006

Oxford Castle
Building Design, *Locked up in luxury*, 2007

King's Cross Regent Quarter
English Heritage, *Capital Solutions*, 2004

Russian Orthodox Cathedral
Building Design, *A Russian resurrection*, 2007

Southwark Cathedral Millennium project
Daily Telegraph, *Romance in the stone,* Giles Worsley, 30 June 2001
Building Design, *A match made in heaven*, Kieran Long, 11 May 2001
Building magazine, *God is in the detail*, 11 May 2001
Church Building Magazine, *Southwark Cathedral,* Ptolemy Dean, issue 70, 2002
NADFAS Review, *The pulling power of Southwark*, Winter 2003
English Heritage, *Capital Solutions*, 2004

St Albans Abbey
English Heritage, *Creativity and Care*, 2009

St Andrews Farnham
Church Building, *Restoring the heart of Farnham*, 2005

St Nicholas Chapel, King's Lynn
Church Building Magazine, April 2016

St Pancras Hotel
Building Design, *Return Ticket*, Oliver Wainwright, 6 May 2011
Architecture Today, *Fit for Purpose*, Gavin Stamp, April 2011
Evening Standard, *Rowan Moore*, 10 Feb 2010
RIBA Journal, *In the footsteps of Scott*, 2007
Sunday Times, Hugh Pearman, 13 March 2011
Wallpaper magazine, *Station master*, 2005

St Paul's Church, Hammersmith
Church Building Magazine, Feb 2012

Sutton House
SPAB News, *Sutton House: Sole Survivor*, Vol. 16, 1995

Valentines Park
London Landscapes, *Back to its best*, 2009

Writings by Richard Griffiths
Unpublished dissertation, *The Houses of West Cambridge*, 1981
ASCHB Transactions, *Early Heating and Ventilating Systems 1790-1850*, 1993
AJ Focus, *Theme: Conservation*, Dec 2002
Building Design, *Reversible Fortunes,* 2004
AJ Specification, Doors and windows issue 2006

Richard Griffiths Architects 1993-2019

Simon Ablett

Jan Alince

Georgina Allison

Michael Asselmeyer

Adrian Azzopardi

Victoria Blackburn

Richard Blight

Rachel Farrer Bristow

Sophie Bromley

Beatrice Carter

Juliet Colman

Ptolemy Dean

Wendy Dellit

Christiana Esteves

Ben Frith

Malcolm Fryer

James Green

Tim Greensmith

Antony Griffiths

Oliver Griffiths

Richard Griffiths

Lucy Grindley

Kathryn Harris

Rebecca Harrison

Udo Heinrich

Richard Hill

Tony Ives

Beatriz Jaime

Naha Johari

Amy Kaspar

Iftikhar Khan

Aya Kihara

Roy Kingston

Eleri Lloyd

Mandy Lorenz

Joanne McClelland

Sophie McIlwaine

Hilary Meth

Sibylle Metge-Toppin

Steven Miller

Jorge Moreira

Raffaele Nannetti

Lily Nicholls

Morgan O'Reilly

Hannah Perkins

Kasia Piernicka

Martina Pozdechova

Lynn Prendergast

Sophie Reeve

Maya Reid

Oliver Reinhold

Julia Ridlington

Pablo Rimoldi

Kirstie Robinson

Penelope Roskell

Patricia Rutherford

Jan Schneidewind

Malcolm Simmonds

Roger Simmons

Ben Slee

Matt Smith

Adam Summerfield

Yanita Todeva

Nicholas Usbey

Debbie Waddington

Kellin Wang

Angus Walker

Anita Walters

Susannah Whitmore

Matthew Wittrick

John Woodcock

Mark Wray

Sutton House enfilade

Velazquez, the Fable of Arachne, Prado (detail)

Drift Barn enfilade

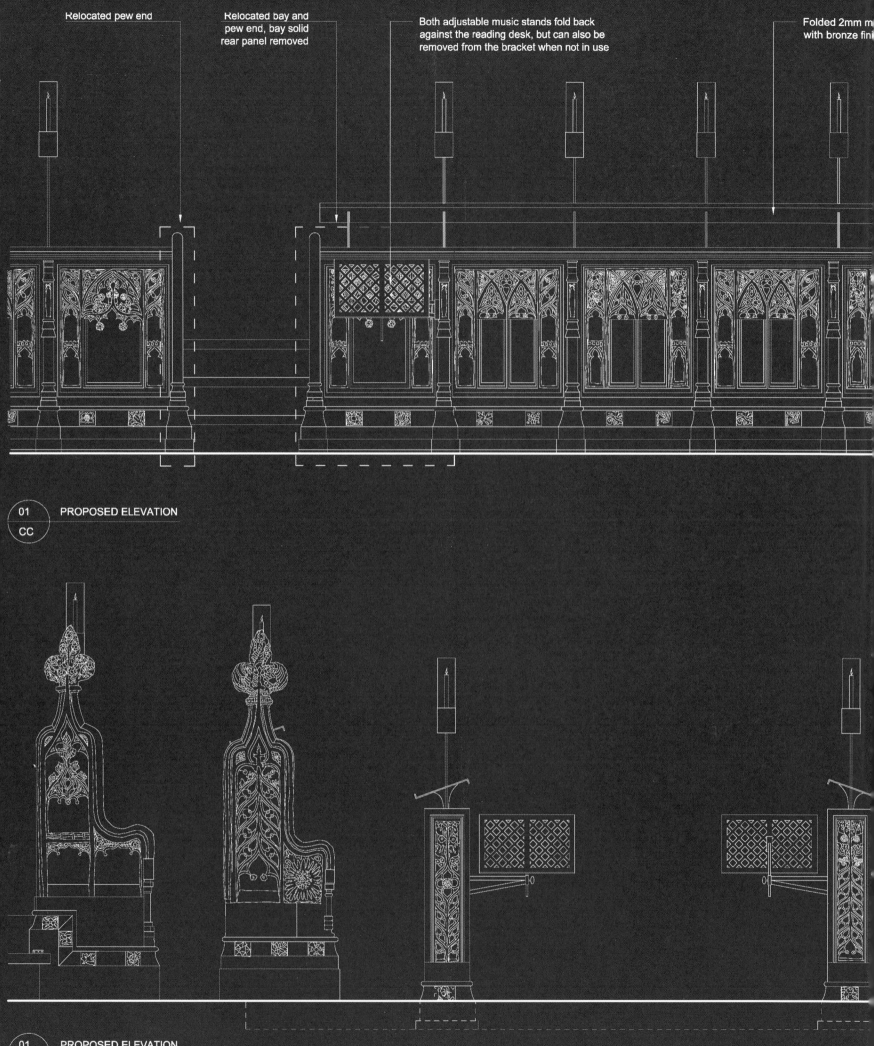

Relocated pew end

Relocated bay and
pew end, bay solid
rear panel removed

Both adjustable music stands fold back
against the reading desk, but can also be
removed from the bracket when not in use

Folded 2mm m
with bronze fini

01   PROPOSED ELEVATION
CC

01   PROPOSED ELEVATION
BB